Use Your
Head

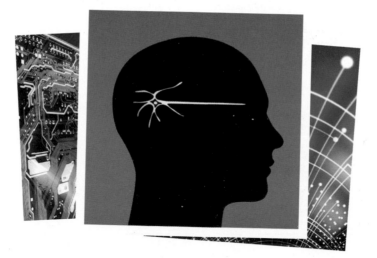

Use Your Head

Head

How to unleash
the power of your mind

Tony Buzan™

and James Harrison, consultant editor

PEARSON

Harlow, England • London • New York • Boston • San Francisco • Toronto • Sydney • Singapore • Hong Kong
Tokyo • Seoul • Taipei • New Delhi • Cape Town • Madrid • Mexico City • Amsterdam • Munich • Paris • Milan

Published by BBC Active, an imprint of Educational Publishers LLP, part of the Pearson Education Group, Edinburgh Gate, Harlow, Essex, CM20 2JE, England.

First published in Great Britain in 2010

ISBN: 978-1-4066-4427-2

British Library Cataloguing-in-Publication Data
A catalogue record for this book is available from the British Library

Library of Congress Cataloging-in-Publication Data
Buzan, Tony.
  Use your head : how to unleash the power of your mind / Tony Buzan, and James Harrison, consultant editor.
    p. cm.
  Includes index.
  ISBN 978-1-4066-4427-2 (pbk.)
  1. Intellect. 2. Memory. 3. Mnemonics. 4. Mental discipline. 5. Thought and thinking. I. Harrison, James, 1954- II. Title.
  BF431.B884 2010
  158.1--dc22
                                2010020845

15
10 9 8 7 6

Designed by Design Deluxe
Typeset in 9.5 Swis721 Lt BT by 30
Printed and bound in Malaysia (CTP-PPSB)

Dedicated to you and to my beloved Mum and Dad,

Jean and Gordon Buzan

Contents

Foreword *Baroness Professor Susan Greenfield* ix

Acknowledgements x

Introduction xii

Part 1 Know your brain 3

1 Your brain is better than you think 5

2 Get inside your head 15

3 IQ and your natural brilliance 27

Part 2 Harness your brain power 39

4 Transform your ability to recall and learn information 41

5 Master mnemonics to double your memory and more 59

6 Energy 'plus' and 'into' memory yields infinite creativity:
$E + M = C^\infty$ 77

Part 3 The essential 'mind tools' for great brains 91

7 Why key words are so important 93

8 Introducing Mind Maps and Radiant Thinking 109

9 How to create a Mind Map 123

10 Speed read to save days, weeks, even months of your time 139

11 The incredible power of 'super' speed reading 151

12 Revolutionise your study skills with the Buzan Organic Study Technique (BOST) 161

Conclusion: Thinking for the future 191

Appendix: Online resources 198

Index 205

Foreword

Physicist Niels Bohr once admonished a student, saying, 'You're not thinking, you're just being logical'. So, I'd like to think that logic is not the criteria by which we evaluate our potential. Our brains are actually very different from 'logical' computers.

In the twenty-first century, it is more important than ever to understand our brains. We are all living longer and healthier lives, but we sometimes forget that there is no point in living longer and healthier lives if we don't keep our brains healthy, too. If we are to have healthy brains, we need to ensure that we keep them active – using our memories, thinking effectively and being creative – to ultimately reach our individual potential, which, not so long ago, was circumscribed by birth and by health; we simply lived out a certain destiny.

Now we are in a position to ask the big questions: 'What am I doing with my life?' 'What is it all about?' I think brain research is 'coming of age' by not just asking how do we make people better or even how do we improve memory – though these are highly welcome developments – but also by tackling the most exciting questions: 'What makes me the individual I am?' 'How can I stretch my potential?'

I applaud Tony for celebrating our brains, especially our twenty-first century brains – something he has been at the forefront of for over 40 years – and the mind. I recommend his highly stimulating *Mind Set* series (*The Mind Map Book*, *The Memory Book*, *The Speed Reading Book* and now *Use Your Head*) of brain improvement books – your adventure is just beginning.

Baroness Professor Susan Greenfield, CBE;
Fullerian Professor of Physiology; Senior Research Fellow,
Lincoln College, University of Oxford; and Holder of the
Ordre National de la Legion d'Honneur

Acknowledgements

Author's acknowledgements

Bringing *Use Your Head* into the twenty-first century, 'the century of the brain', has been a global team effort and I would like to extend my heartfelt appreciation to the entire network of Buzan Centres International, now well and truly established – and growing! Thank you to all the Buzan master trainers and licensed instructors from Buzan World, including Masanori Kanda, Mikiko Chikada Kawase, Ken Ito and Shiro Kobayashi in Japan; Bill Jarrard and Jennifer Goddard at Buzan Centre Australia/NZ; Henry Toi, Eric Cheong, Thum Cheng Cheong and the Buzan Asia team; Hilde Jaspaert at Buzan Europe; and Jorge O. Castañeda, President, Buzan Latin America.

Thank you also to Brian Lee for being a friend and stalwart in helping me to bring the *Mind Set* series to the public; to Phil Chambers, World Mind Mapping champion and senior Buzan Licensed Instructor for his superb Mind Map creations and tireless backroom input (contact **www.learning-tech.co.uk**). My heartfelt thanks also to my brother, Barry Buzan, and artist Lorraine Gill. Thank you also to my 'home team' at Buzan HQ, including Anne Reynolds, Suzi Rockett and Jenny Redman for their superb logistical support and effort.

At Pearson, my publisher, I would like to thank Richard Stagg, director, who was a prime figure in the launching of this project; and add my profound thanks to Samantha Jackson, my cherished commissioning editor, for her total commitment to *Use Your Head* throughout its long gestation. Also to her team in Harlow, Caroline Jordan and Emma Devlin. My thanks are completed by acknowledging also James Harrison, my independent consultant editor, for helping to shape, structure and nail everything together throughout the project. James has also added becoming a Buzan Licensed Instructor in Mind Mapping and iMindMap Master Trainer to his credits.

Finally my thanks, too, to all those Mind Mappers, mnemonists and speed readers who enthusiastically provided stories and tests, for both the first edition and this revised and updated edition, as well as those who, for reasons of space, I have either omitted to thank or have been unable to include.

Publisher's acknowledgements

We are grateful to the following for giving their permission to reproduce copyright material.

Mind Maps

The Mind Maps remain the copyright of their owners, as listed below:

Phil Chambers pages 33, 62, 63, 65, 66, 84, 120 and 131, Bob Harvey page 73, Robert Walster page 103, Hilde Jaspaert page 126, Alan Burton pages 134, 135 and 137 and Suzi Rockett page 143.

Photographs

Edward Hughes pages 11 and 12.

Images

Original black and white illustrations by A1 Creative Services, Lorraine Gill, Mike Gilkes, Pep Reiff, Robert Walster, Alan Burton and Ben Cracknell Studios (all redrawn by Phil Chambers for this edition).

Figure 2.2 courtesy of MedicalRF.com/Science Photo Library; Figure 2.3 courtesy of Mike Agliolo/Science Photo Library; Figure 5.3 © Salvador Dalí, Fundació Gala-Salvador Dalí, DACS, 2010 and Bettman/CORBIS; Figure 6.1 courtesy of Phil Chambers; Figure 6.2 © Getty Images/Stuart Gregory; Figure 6.3 courtesy of POD/Photodisc, photograph by Steve Cole; Figure 6.5 courtesy of POD/Photodisc; Figure 10.2 courtesy of POD/Jupiter Images, Brand X, Alamy.

Every effort has been made by the publisher to obtain permission from the appropriate sources to reproduce material that appears in this book. In some instances, we may have been unable to trace the owners of copyright material and would appreciate any information that would enable us to do so.

Introduction

Imagine that you are an Olympic athlete, muscularly fit, incredibly flexible and – in cardiovascular terms – in good condition … and you get bogged down in a swamp or quicksand. What would you be thinking? Invariably, that the way to get out of this situation is to use your Olympian energy. What will happen to you if you do that? You will sink fast.

Therein, as Shakespeare said, lies the rub. There is the essence of the dilemma. Despite being intelligent, powerful and focused, you, the Olympic athlete, would sink because you didn't apply the right thinking to the challenge you faced. You would sink despite and, indeed, *because* of your *very best efforts*. That is what so many of us do when it comes to using our brains – we, unknowingly, don't know how to access and apply its immense powers.

Use Your Head has been written to help you understand how to use the power of your brain successfully, no matter what challenge you face. I call it the 'operations manual' for your brain. It is designed to help you nurture your 'super-biocomputer' and unleash the natural and extraordinary range of mental skills that you possess.

Let me now tell you one simple story about how I came to develop this 'brain manual' …

I was at university, my marks were slip-sliding away, my confidence was slip-sliding away and the work I had to do was piling up. So, in desperation, I went to the library and spoke to the librarian (in hushed tones).

'I need a book on how to use my brain.'

She said:

'The medical section is over there.'

I said:

'I don't want to *operate* on it, I want to learn how to *use* it.'

She said,

'Oh, there are no books on that.'

That was it.

I thought, how amazing! If you purchase a laptop or mobile phone or other PDA, what do you get with it?

A MANUAL (either hard copy or online).

Where, though, was the operations manual for the most important piece of equipment imaginable? There was none. Today there is and I am delighted to introduce to you the much-needed operation manual for the brain – namely, *Use Your Head*.

In 1974, the BBC launched my ten-part television series *Use Your Head* and first formally introduced to the world my basic concept of the Mind Map®. *Use Your Head* was the 'tie-in' book and really the 'mother' of my brain books (which later included *The Memory Book*, *The Mind Map Book*, and *The Speed Reading Book*). The television series was repeated regularly for ten years and the book of the same name became a worldwide bestseller, launching me as a brand and my hugely popular seminars around the globe.

By the end of the 1970s, the first success stories were being reported – especially the amazing, inspirational story of Edward Hughes (see page 8). In the early 1980s, the first of an ongoing series of super-lectures to large bodies of students were given. Among the most notable of these was the Soweto 2000 event in Johannesburg, South Africa, when 2000 teenagers from the township of Soweto attended, voluntarily, a three-day *Use Your Head* spectacular.

On 21 April 1995, *Use Your Head* 'came of age', with its twenty-first birthday, having already surpassed worldwide sales of over a million copies. To mark the occasion, the biggest celebration ever held for a book – the Festival of the Mind, a twenty-first birthday party – was held at the Royal Albert Hall in London (see Figure I.1).

As we entered the new millennium, the Waterstones book chain, in conjunction with the Express Newspaper Group, selected *Use Your Head* as one of their 1000 greatest books of the second millennium and recommended that it be in all libraries of the coming 'millennium of the mind'.

Figure I.1 **Celebrations at the first Festival of the Mind, held in London's Royal Albert Hall in 1995, to mark 21 years since the first publication of Use Your Head**

To mark the fact that more than 35 years have passed since its initial publication, the BBC has launched *The Mind Set* series – the first encyclopedia about the use of the brain, which features my updated version of *Use Your Head*, as well as its 'children', *The Memory Book*, *The Mind Map Book* and *The Speed Reading Book*. You now hold in your hands the latest version of that very book and will, I hope, benefit from it in the same way that millions have already done. It will show you how to use your 'manager of knowledge', your brain, and how to get the maximum from it, in terms of learning, memory and creativity.

Creativity is of special concern to me because it seems that our learning systems are designed to *drum out* creativity! Controlled creativity studies prove this. Groups of people of different ages were given problems to solve. They were then examined in detail to assess how well they performed, how fast, flexible, imaginative and original they were. A percentage score was given for their 'creativity potential'. The findings were fascinating (see Figure I.2):

- the first group tested were nursery school children – they scored 95 per cent

- primary school children scored 75 per cent

- secondary school pupils scored 50 per cent

- university students scored 25 per cent.

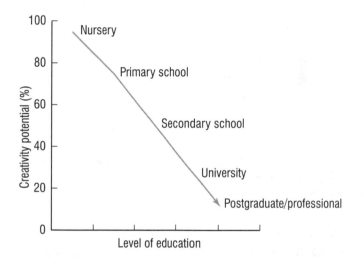

Figure I.2 **Graph showing how our creativity potential, as a percentage, decreases dramatically as we age – the education system kicking in and kicking out our creativity**

That is a massive drop in creativity, which is continued into adult-hood. The findings apparently show that, as we get older, creativity appears to decline still further.

All this is normal. As the average age of the population is increasing, therefore the average amount of creativity per person is decreasing globally. It means, though, that we need to handle the world's major source of wealth – intelligence – better. The *Harvard*

Business Review was clearly convinced of this when, at the beginning of the twenty-first century, it featured the words 'The looming creativity crisis' on its front cover.

The good news is that 'normal' is not *natural*. Normal is the result of inappropriate training that is unwittingly designed to decrease creativity. At any age, your creativity should be rising. *Use Your Head* will help you to achieve this increase in creativity and all aspects of brain power for the rest of your life.

How to use this book

By the time you have finished this book you will understand much more about how your brain works and how to increase the power of your memory, how to use it creatively to the best advantage, how to Mind Map more effectively, how to read faster and more efficiently and how to optimise your study and work techniques.

The book is dividend into easily manageable parts and, within each part, there are easily digestible chapters.

Part 1 takes you on a journey inside your brain, providing an easy-to-follow guide, and gives you a fascinating insight into the different aspects of your brain's functioning. It explores the concepts of intelligence and IQ, multiple intelligences, the way your brain gathers intelligence and how you see the world through your mind's eye. It goes on to examine how the natural way to learn and traditional learning systems often do not co-exist harmoniously, which is fundamentally important if you are going to *learn how to learn* before learning about any subject.

Part 2 introduces you to the core skills inherent in learning: memory and creativity. It explores how your brain manages to remember, learn and understand, explains how you recall *during* and *after* learning and introduces several key mnemonic techniques and tests.

Part 3 gets to grips with the 'mind tools' you need to boost your brainpower, including the ultimate thinking tool – the Mind Map. Called the 'Swiss Army knife for the brain', the Mind Map taps into your brain's natural tendencies to think in images, in colour and network radiantly, rather than make links in a linear fashion.

After exploring your mind's internal 'maps', the way you think is applied to the way in which you can use language, words, imagery and Mind Maps for recording, organising, remembering, creative thinking and problem solving.

How to prepare and create Mind Maps is then fully explained, after which you are introduced to the technique of speed reading – a skill that will dramatically increase your reading speed and your comprehension at the same time.

Managing information is critical for study and business skills. This section also deals with the new Buzan Organic Study Technique (BOST®), which will enable you to study any subject and apply it to managing learning, analysing, prioritising and presenting information. The final chapter looks at how far and fast we have moved forwards in understanding our brains and the applications of the manager of knowledge, the brain, in the 'age of intelligence'.

At various stages in the book I have included exercises and suggestions for further activity. By practising these exercises and activities, you will have the opportunity to really stretch your mind and train your brain.

Finally, at the back of the book, you will find a comprehensive online resources section.

Use Your Head has been designed to help you expand as an individual, primarily in the areas of reading, noting taking and note making and studying, though you will find that the complete application is much wider. By using what you learn in *Use Your Head*, you will gather an increasing awareness of yourself and be able to develop your own ways of thinking. When you have finished and reviewed the book, browse through it again to see in which other areas of your life the information can be helpfully applied.

Remember, we all start with different levels of learning ability and progress at the pace best suited to us. It is important to measure your improvement primarily in relation to yourself rather than other people. You should therefore work out your own schedule for practising and studying, keeping to it as firmly as possible.

So, let's begin the journey into innovative learning and thinking techniques to fulfil your mental potential and help you ... *use your head!*

Your brain has physcial **beauty** and **complexity**, and has **enormous intellectual** and **emotional powers**.

TONY BUZAN

Part 1

Know your brain

There really is no doubt that your brain is capable of infinitely more complex tasks than has been thought.

Part 1 looks at the latest findings about our brains and sheds light on a number of the areas in which performance and self-realisation can be achieved.

Your brain is better than you think

What happens in your brain when you eat a pear, smell flowers, listen to music, watch a river, touch a loved one or simply remember something?

The answer is both simple and incredibly complex.

Each piece of information entering your brain – each feeling, remembrance, thought (including each word, number, code, nutrient, perfume, line, colour, image, pulse, note and texture) – can be represented as a central sphere, from which radiate dozens, hundreds, thousands, *millions* of hooks. Each hook represents an association and each association has its own infinite number of connections. The number of associations you have already used can be regarded as your memory, database or library. You can be sure that in the mind now reading this passage lies a data management system that makes the analytical and storage capacities of the fastest supercomputer in the world (currently the IBM Roadrunner of Los Alamos National Laboratory) look tiny by comparison.

The thinking structure of your brain can therefore be considered a gigantic branching association machine (BAM) – a biological supercomputer where thinking radiates from a truly infinite number of data nodes. This structure reflects your neural networks, which make up the physical architecture of your brain. In fact, your existing database is founded on the fact that a single neuron can make 10^{28} connections.

It is only in recent years that scientists have begun to discover the true potential of our brains. By learning more about your own brain, you can discover the unique capabilities of your mind and discover that being 'only human', far from being an admission of failure, is an incredible statement (see also page 36)! We have to learn how our brains operate in order to make the most of our extraordinary capabilities.

Your brain's true potential – your mind's unique possibilities

Since I wrote the first chapter on the brain for the first edition of *Use Your Head*, research in that area has been exploding with new and exciting discoveries. Rather than stating, as I did then, that 'only in the last 150 years' has the bulk of progress been made in this area, I can now say that only in the last 30 years has the bulk of our knowledge been accumulated. That seems extraordinarily recent when you consider life appeared on Earth 4,500,000 years ago. Bear in mind, however, that we have known the location of our brains for only the last 500 years.

In some ways, this is not surprising. Imagine for a moment that you have no idea where your brain is to be found and a friend asks, 'Where is the centre of your feelings, emotions, thoughts, memories, drives and desires located?' You, like most others (including Aristotle!) might quite rationally decide that your brain is located in the heart and stomach area, because that is where you experience the direct physical manifestation of mental activity most regularly and dramatically.

Even now, as neuroscientists pursue with CAT scans and electron microscopes what must be the most elusive quarry the human race has ever chased, they must still admit that the sum total of our knowledge of the human mind is probably less than 1 per cent of what there is to know. Just when tests seem to prove that the mind works in a given way, along comes another test showing a different picture or along comes another human being with a brain who manages to make us need to rework the whole frame.

This has been amply demonstrated in the field of memory. For example, in 1991, at the time of the first World Memory Championship, a shuffled pack of cards could be memorised and recalled accurately by a good contender after around five minutes cogitation. When Dominic O'Brien smashed the record with a time of 2 minutes 29 seconds at those championships, experts promptly pronounced this to be near the limit of human capacity. A decade and a half later, recalling a complete shuffled pack was down to around 30 seconds. Then, in 2007, Ben Pridmore broke that mental barrier by 3.72 seconds. His achievement pushed back, to a gigantic degree, the boundaries of human mental capacity.

To cite further examples, it is evident that most of the more scientific disciplines, despite their apparent differences of direction, are all being drawn into a whirlpool, the centre of which is the brain. Chemists are now involved with the intricate chemical structures that exist and interact inside our heads; biologists are uncovering the brain's biological functions; physicists are finding parallels with their investigations into the farthest reaches of space; psychologists are trying to pin the mind down and finding the experience frustratingly like trying to place a finger on a little globule of mercury; and mathematicians, who have constructed models for complex computers and even for the universe itself, still can't come up with a formula for the operations that go on regularly inside each of our heads every day of our lives.

What we are gathering, therefore, from our efforts at the moment is the knowledge that the brain is infinitely more subtle and capable than we had previously thought. Also, everyone who has what is ironically called a 'normal' brain has much more ability and potential than was previously believed.

I would like now to present a classic and fabulous example of the infinite possibilities of the mind made manifest.

An impossible dream – the Edward Hughes story

After *Use Your Head* was first published in 1974, a 'fairly average student, middle of the form, not doing particularly well in any subject' took, in 1982, at the age of 15, his A level examinations. His results, as expected, and as they had always been, were Cs and Bs. He was disappointed with the results because he had set his heart on going to Cambridge University and realised that if he carried on academically the way he was, then he didn't stand a chance.

The student's name was Edward Hughes.

A little while later, Edward's father, George, introduced him to *Use Your Head* and, armed with new information about himself and about how to Mind Map, learn and study, Edward went back to school revitalised and motivated. He announced that he was going for As in all his subjects and definitely wanted to be put forward for Cambridge.

The reactions of his teachers were understandably bemused and varied. 'You can't be serious: come on, you've got no chance – your academic results have never been anywhere near the standard that Cambridge requires', said one. 'Don't be daft! You could possibly get a B, but you'll probably get a C', said the second. When Edward said that he wished to take not only the standard exam but also write the scholarship paper, his teacher said flatly, 'No, it's a waste of the school's money and your time entering for that exam. We don't think you'll pass as the exams are very, very difficult – we don't even get many passes from our best candidates.' After Edward persisted, the school was willing to put him forward, but he had to pay his own considerable entrance fee in order to not 'waste the school's money'.

Meanwhile, a third teacher said that he had been teaching the same subject for the last 12 years, he was the expert in the area and knew what he was talking about when he said Hughes would only get a B or a C. The teacher named 'another chap' who was a much better student than Edward and said Edward would never be as good as him. As Edward said at the time, 'I disagreed with his reading of the situation!' A fourth teacher chuckled, said that he obviously admired Edward's ambition, his dream was possible but unlikely, even if he worked hard he'd only get a B, but wished him luck and said he always liked someone who showed a bit of initiative.

'I will get an A'

To each of the teachers, and to anyone who questioned his goals, Edward's final response was always simply, 'I will get an A'.

Initially, the school did not want to put Edward's name forward for Cambridge, but, after a while, agreed to do so, letting the colleges at Cambridge know that they didn't really think this particular student was likely to get the place for which he applied. The next and immediate stage was the college interviews. At these, the Cambridge dons informed Edward of the school's opinion of him, agreed with the school that his probability of success was very low, admired his initiative, told him he'd need at least two Bs and an A, but more probably two As and a B, or three As, and wished him luck.

Still undaunted, Edward pursued a plan of *Use Your Head* and physical training. In his own words:

I was getting nearer the exams. I summarised my last two years of school notes neatly into Mind Maps. I then coloured them, highlighted them and produced giant master Mind Maps for each of the courses and, in some instances, for each major section of each course. In this way I could see where and how the more detailed elements fitted together and, in addition, get a good overview, thus enabling me to just flick through giant sections of the course with completely accurate recall.

I kept reviewing these Mind Maps once a week and, as it got nearer to the exams, even more regularly. I practised my recall Mind Maps, not looking at my books or other notes, simply drawing from my memory what knowledge and understanding of the subjects I had, and then comparing these Mind Maps with my master Mind Maps, checking the differences.

I also made sure that I had read all the main key books and then sorted these down to a few, read them in depth and Mind Mapped them so that my understanding and memory were maximised. In addition, I studied good essay form and style and used my own Mind Maps as a basis for practising essay and examination writing.

I accompanied this by getting fitter, by running two to three miles, two to three times per week, getting lots of fresh air, doing lots of press-ups and sit-ups and working out in a gym. I became better physically, which I found helped my concentration enormously. As they say, healthy body, healthy mind; healthy mind, healthy body. I felt better about myself and I felt better about my work.

The examinations – the results

Eventually, Edward sat four examinations: geography, the geography scholarship paper, medieval history and business studies. His results were as follows:

Subject	Mark	Rank
Geography	A	Top student
Geography scholarship	Distinction	Top student
Medieval history	A	Top student
Business studies	A and 2 distinctions	Top student ever

Within a day of the publication of the results, Edward's first-choice college at Cambridge had confirmed his place and accepted his request for a year off to see a bit of the world before he started his university course.

At Cambridge

In terms of sport, Edward was immediately successful, playing in his college's football, tennis and squash teams.

In the area of student societies, he might even be termed an overachiever for, in addition to founding the Young Entrepreneurs Society – the largest of its kind in Europe – he was asked to preside over the Very Nice Society – a charitable society of 3600 members, which grew to 4500 under his presidency, making it the largest society in the history of the university. In view of his work for the two societies, the other society presidents asked Edward to form and preside over a society for presidents. That he did and became president of Presidents Club!

Figure 1.1 Edward Hughes during his time at Cambridge University, where he founded the Young Entrepreneurs Society

Academically, he first studied the habits of the 'average student' and reported:

They spent about 12–13 hours reading for each essay, linearly noting all the information they could, reading all possible books, after which they'd spend three to four hours writing the essay itself (some students would actually rewrite their essays, occasionally spending an entire week on one essay).

In view of his experience with the A level preparation and examinations, Edward decided to allocate himself two to three hours a day, five days a week, to study.

During those three hours I went to a key lecture, summarising all the relevant information in Mind Map form. I set myself the goal that, as soon as any essays were set, I'd go away and do a Mind Map on what I knew about the subject or what I thought was relevant and then leave it for a couple of days, think about it, turn it over in my mind and then speed and range read the relevant books, Mind Mapping the relevant information from them. I'd then take a break or do some exercise and then come back and do a Mind Map on the essay itself. Having completed my essay plan, I'd take another break and then sit down and complete the essay, always within 45 minutes. With this technique I regularly achieved high marks.

Before the final Cambridge examinations, Edward worked to a schedule virtually identical to that he had used to prepare for his A levels, and then took six final examinations.

The results

In the first examination, he was given a pass – normally considered fair, but excellent here because 50 per cent of those taking the examination failed it and no firsts were given. In the second, third and fourth, he achieved three 2.1s and, in the final exams, two firsts – not only firsts, but *starred* firsts, which are the highest marks in the university for those subjects.

Immediately after graduation, Edward was offered employment as a strategic thinker for a multinational entrepreneurial company – a job described by the university as 'one of the best ever' for a Cambridge graduate. As Edward summarised:

> *Cambridge was fantastic. I was fortunate enough to get a lot out of it – a lot of friends, a lot of experience, a lot of physical activity, a lot of enthusiasm for and success in academia and three years of absolutely great enjoyment. The major difference between myself and the others was simply that I knew how to think – how to use my head. I was a C and B student before I knew how to 'get an A'. I did it. Anyone can.*

Edward Hughes today

After graduating from Cambridge, Edward worked in London for two years before applying to go to a business school. At the time, the top MBAs were from Harvard and Stanford. He was accepted by both, but chose Harvard based on its international reputation.

At Harvard, while again being active in societies and sport, he excelled academically. He was a Baker Scholar – a prestigious award given to the top 5 per cent of students at the Harvard Business School.

Post Harvard, he has led a successful business career and has been CEO of several companies. He is married to an Australian who was a professional squash player and they have two beautiful teenage children. They live in San Diego, California, which is often regarded as having the best weather in the world. Edward is the CEO of a nanotechnology company, a member of the Young Presidents Organisation and on the boards of several charities. He remains an active sportsman and is a scratch golfer.

To this day he uses Mind Maps and many of the study techniques he learned from *Use Your Head*. He is particularly pleased that his children are being taught to use Mind Maps at school and hopes their teachers will be more open-minded regarding their unlimited potential than his own teachers were.

Get inside your head

Your brain is a mass consisting of 78 per cent water, 10 per cent fat and around 8 per cent protein. It weighs around 1.5 kilos and it looks rather like a walnut. It also represents roughly 2 per cent of your total bodyweight, but consumes 20 per cent of your calories. The more you think, the more calories you burn.

The cerebral cortex

Divided into two parts – the left and right hemispheres – the soft mass of the cerebral cortex represents 80 per cent of the total weight of your brain. The two hemispheres are connected by a 'cable' consisting of more than 250 million nerve fibres – the *corpus callosum*. It ensures efficient communication between the two hemispheres and, indeed, any human activity requires an intense collaboration between them. The soft part of your brain is covered by a thin layer called the *cortex*, which consists of nerve cells. In this layer, which is no thicker than three human hairs, are located most of your cerebral processes – thinking, memory, speech and muscular movement.

From the moment you were born, both hemispheres started to specialise, with tasks being divided between them. This is called the *lateralisation process*.

More than one brain

Neuroscience studies have shown that this division of tasks is unique to each individual, but some common features exist for most human beings.

It all started back in the late 1960s and early 1970s, when research was begun that was to change the history of our appreciation of the human brain and eventually won Roger Sperry of the California Institute of Technology a Nobel Prize and Robert Ornstein worldwide fame for his work on brainwaves and specialisation of function. That work has been carried on through the 1980s by Professor Eran Zaidel and others.

In summary, what Sperry and Ornstein discovered was that the two sides of your brain, or your two *cortices*, linked by a fantastically complex network of nerve fibres (the corpus callosum), deal, dominantly, with different types of mental activity.

In most people, the *left cortex* deals with logic, words, lists, number, linearity, analysis and so on – the so-called 'academic' activities. While the left cortex is engaged in these activities, the right cortex is more in the 'alpha wave' or resting state, ready to assist. The *right cortex* deals with rhythm, imagination, colour, daydreaming, spatial awareness, Gestalt (completing tendency) and dimension.

Subsequent research has shown that when people are encouraged to develop a mental area they had previously considered weak, this development, rather than detracting from other areas, seems to produce a synergetic effect, with all areas of mental performance improving.

At first glance, history seemed to deny this finding however, for most of the 'great brains' appeared very lopsided in mental terms: Einstein and other great scientists seemed to be predominantly 'left cortex' dominant, while Picasso, Cézanne and Beethoven and other great artists and musicians appeared to be 'right cortex' dominant. A more thorough investigation unearthed some fascinating truths, however. Einstein failed French at school and numbered among his activities playing the violin, art, sailing and imagination games!

Einstein gave credit for many of his more significant scientific insights to his imagination games. While daydreaming on a hill one summer day, he imagined riding sunbeams to the far extremities of the universe and, on finding himself returned, 'illogically', to the surface of the sun, he realised that the universe must indeed be curved and his previous 'logical' training was incomplete. The numbers, equations and words he wrapped around this new image gave us his theory of relativity – a synthesis of the left and right cortexes.

Similarly, the great artists have turned out to be 'whole-brained'. Rather than notebooks filled with stories of drunken parties and paint slapped haphazardly to produce masterpieces, entries similar to the following have been found:

> *Up at 6 a.m. Spent seventeenth day on painting number six of the latest series. Mixed four parts orange with two parts yellow to produce a colour combination which I placed in upper left-hand corner of canvas, to act in visual opposition to spiral structures in lower right-hand corner, producing desired balance in eye of perceiver.*

A telling example of just how much left-cortex activity goes into what we normally consider right-cortex pursuits.

In addition to the research of Sperry and Ornstein, the experimental evidence of increased overall performance and the confirming historical fact that many 'great brains' were indeed using both ranges of their capacity, one man in the last thousand years stands out as a supreme example of what a human being can do if both cortical sides of the brain are developed simultaneously: Leonardo da Vinci.

The other Da Vinci code

In his time, Leonardo da Vinci was arguably the most accomplished man in each of the following disciplines: art, sculpture, physiology, general science, architecture, mechanics, anatomy, physics, invention, meteorology, geology, engineering and aviation. He could also play, compose and sing spontaneous ballads when given any stringed instrument in the courts of Europe.

Rather than separating these different areas of his latent ability, he combined them. Leonardo's scientific notebooks are filled with three-dimensional drawings and images. Just as interesting is the fact that the final plans for his great painting masterpieces often look like architectural plans, including as they do straight lines, angles, curves and numbers incorporating mathematics, logic and precise measurements in his visual 'notes'.

It seems, then, that when we describe ourselves as talented in certain areas and not in others, what we are really describing is those areas of our potential we have successfully developed and those others still lying dormant, which, in reality, could, with the right nurturing, flourish.

Figure 2.1 shows an inventory of cerebral processes and which hemisphere is most involved when we carry them out.

The findings relating to the right and left cortices give added support to the work you will be doing on memory systems, note taking and communication, as well as advanced Mind Mapping, for in each of these areas it is essential to use both sides of your brain.

Your brain's 'superhighways'

In your brain, there are a minimum of a million million individual *neurons*, which are nerve cells – that's roughly the number of stars in the Milky Way! This figure becomes even more astounding when you realise that each of your neurons can interact with from 1 to 100,000 other neurons in many ways.

A neuron is a specialist nerve cell that transmits electrical signals. Neurons do not work individually but are connected in circuits, allowing the body to transmit sensory and motor signals in all regions of the body.

Neurons have three main parts: a single cell body, one axon and many dendrites. The role of the *dendrites* is to receive the information and make contacts with other neurons, thus allowing the transmission of electrical impulses. The *axon* is the filiform extension of the nerve cell from the cell body. The axon is covered with a myelin coating and is in charge of sending signals to other neurons. Most neurons have many dendrites and one single axon.

Neurons use their highly specialist structure to send and receive signals. Each individual neuron receives information from thousands of other neurons and forwards the information to thousands of other neurons. Information is relayed from one neuron to the other thanks to *neurotransmission*. This indirect process takes

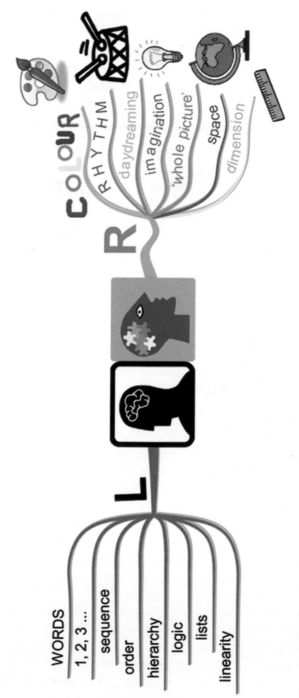

Figure 2.1 Mind Map showing how the right and left sides of the cortex have different dominant processes

place in the space between the nerve ending and the dendrites of the next cell. This space is called a 'synaptic gap' or *synapse*. The connection between two neurons is called a *synaptic connection*.

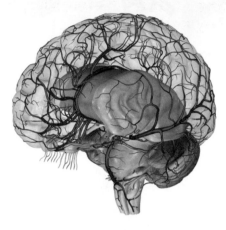

Figure 2.2 **The human brain**

Source: MedicalRF.com/SciencePhotoLibrary

Synaptic connections: the mental events

What is the relevance of all of this to learning, thinking and memory? It has long been proven that the number of synaptic connections linked to specific data determines the quality of its retention – that is, the more simultaneous connections there are when storing something, the higher is the probability of retrieving them afterwards.

Every time you have a thought, the biochemical/electromagnetic resistance along the pathway carrying that thought is reduced. It is like trying to clear a path through a forest. The first time is a struggle because you have to fight your way through the undergrowth. The second time you travel that way will be easier because of the path you cleared on your first journey. The more times you travel that path, the less resistance there will be until, after many repetitions, you have a wide, smooth track that requires little or no clearing. A similar thing happens in your brain, so, the more you repeat patterns or maps of thought, the less resistance there is to them. Also – and this is of greater significance – repetition in itself increases the probability of repetition. In other words, the more times a 'mental event' happens, the more likely it is to happen again.

Interconnections between your brain's 'little grey cells'

At the time I was writing the first edition of *Use Your Head*, in 1973, it had been estimated that the number of brain cell permutations might be as many as 1 followed by 800 noughts. To realise just how enormous that number is, compare it with a mathematical fact about the universe, that one of the smallest items in the universe is the atom (see Figure 2.3).

Figure 2.3 An atom – one of the tiniest entities known. In the tip of your finger there are many billions of atoms and, in the entire universe, a number equal to 10 with 100 noughts after it

Source: Mike Agliolo/Science Photo Library

The biggest thing we know is the universe itself (see Figure 2.4).

The number of atoms in the known universe is predictably enormous: 10 with 100 noughts after it (see Figure 2.5). The number of possible thought maps in one brain makes even this number seem tiny (see Figure 2.6).

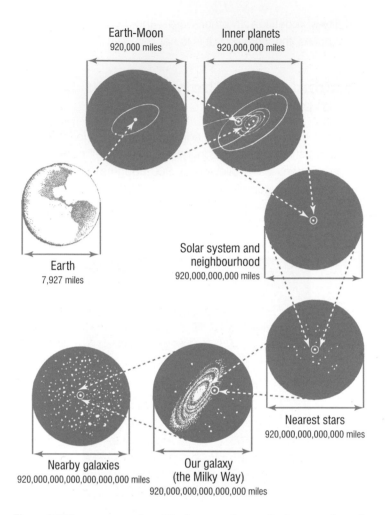

Earth-Moon
920,000 miles

Inner planets
920,000,000 miles

Earth
7,927 miles

Solar system and neighbourhood
920,000,000,000 miles

Nearest stars
920,000,000,000,000 miles

Nearby galaxies
920,000,000,000,000,000,000 miles

**Our galaxy
(the Milky Way)**
920,000,000,000,000,000 miles

Figure 2.4 The enormous size of the known universe. Each successive sphere is a thousand million times (1,000,000,000) as big as the one before it

10, 000, 000, 000, 000, 000, 000, 000, 000, 000, 000, 000, 000,
000, 000, 000, 000, 000, 000, 000, 000, 000, 000, 000, 000, 000,
000, 000, 000, 000, 000, 000, 0

Figure 2.5 The number of atoms – one of the smallest particles we know of – in the known universe – the largest thing we know of

1, 000, 000, 000, 000, 000, 000, 000, 000, 000, 000, 000, 000, 000,
000, 000, 000, 000, 000, 000, 000, 000, 000, 000, 000, 000, 000, 000,
000, 000, 000, 000, 000, 000, 000, 000, 000, 000, 000, 000, 000, 000,
000, 000, 000, 000, 000, 000, 000, 000, 000, 000, 000, 000, 000, 000,
000, 000, 000, 000, 000, 000, 000, 000, 000, 000, 000, 000, 000, 000,
000, 000, 000, 000, 000, 000, 000, 000, 000, 000, 000, 000, 000, 000,
000, 000, 000, 000, 000, 000, 000, 000, 000, 000, 000, 000, 000, 000,
000, 000, 000, 000, 000, 000, 000, 000, 000, 000, 000, 000, 000, 000,
000, 000, 000, 000, 000, 000, 000, 000, 000, 000, 000, 000, 000, 000,
000, 000, 000, 000, 000, 000, 000, 000, 000, 000, 000, 000, 000, 000,
000, 000, 000, 000, 000, 000, 000, 000, 000, 000, 000, 000, 000, 000,
000, 000, 000, 000, 000, 000, 000, 000, 000, 000, 000, 000, 000, 000,
000, 000, 000, 000, 000, 000, 000, 000, 000, 000, 000, 000, 000, 000,
000, 000, 000, 000, 000, 000, 000, 000, 000, 000, 000, 000, 000, 000,
000, 000, 000, 000, 000, 000, 000, 000, 000, 000, 000, 000, 000, 000,
000, 000, 000, 000, 000, 000, 000, 000, 000, 000, 000, 000, 000, 000,
000, 000, 000, 000, 000, 000, 000, 000, 000, 000, 000, 000, 000, 000,
000, 000, 000, 000, 000, 000, 000, 000, 000, 000, 000, 000, 000, 000,
000, 000, 000, 000, 000, 000, 000, 000, 000, 000, 000, 000, 000, 000,
000, 00

Figure 2.6 In the late 1960s, it was calculated that the number of different patterns the 1,000,000,000,000 individual nerve cells in your brain could make was 1 followed by 800 noughts, but recent estimates have shown that even this number is too small

Shortly after the first edition of *Use Your Head* was published, Dr Pyotr Anokhin of Moscow University, who had spent the last few years of his life studying the information processing capabilities of the brain, stated that the number 1 followed by 800 noughts was a gross underestimation. The new number he had calculated was conservative, due to the relative clumsiness of our current measuring instruments in comparison with the incredible delicacy of the brain. The number he came up with was not 1 followed by 800 noughts. Dr Anokhin stated:

> The pattern-making capability of the brain, or 'degrees of freedom' throughout the brain, is so great that writing it would take a line of figures, in normal manuscript characters, more than 10.5 million kilometres in length! With such a number of possibilities, the brain is a keyboard on which hundreds of millions of different melodies – acts of behaviour or

intelligence – can be played. No man yet exists or has existed who has even approached using his full brain. We accept no limitations on the power of the brain – it is limitless.

Use Your Head has been written to help you play your infinite mental keyboard.

Models of perception: eye, brain, camera

First, let us consider the eye/brain/mind system. As recently as 60 years ago, the camera provided the model for our perception and mental imaging – the lens of the camera corresponding to the lens of the eye and the photographic plate to the brain itself. This conception was held for some time but was very inadequate. You can confirm this inadequacy by doing the following exercises.

In the way that we normally do when daydreaming, close your eyes and imagine your favourite object. Having clearly registered the image on your inner eye, perform the following activities:

- rotate it in front of you

- look at it from the top

- look at it from underneath

- change its colour at least three times

- move it away, as if seen from a long distance

- bring it close again

- make it gigantic

- make it tiny

- totally change the shape of it

- make it disappear

- bring it back.

These feats can be performed by you without much difficulty; the apparatus and machinery of a camera could not even begin to perform them (see Figure 2.7).

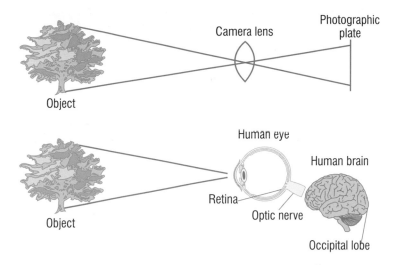

Figure 2.7 **Contrary to earlier thought, the brain operates in a much more complex manner than a camera**

The hologram as a model of the brain

Developments in more refined technology have fortunately given us a much better analogy than the camera: the hologram.

To create a hologram, an especially concentrated light or laser beam is split into two. One half of the ray is directed towards the plate, while the other half is bounced off the image and then directed back towards the other half of the ray. The special holographic plate records the millions of fragments into which the rays shatter when they collide. When this plate is held up in front of the laser beams directed at special angles towards it, the original image is recreated. Amazingly, it is not recreated as a flat picture on the plate, but is perfectly duplicated as a three-dimensional ghost object that hangs in space. If the object is looked at from above, below or the side, it is seen in exactly the same way as the original object would have been seen (see Figure 2.8).

Even more amazingly, if the original holographic plate is rotated through 90 degrees, as many as 90 images can be recorded on the same plate without interfering with each other.

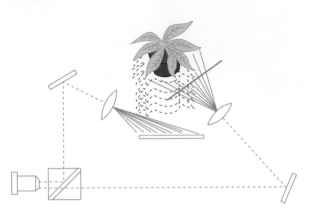

*Figure 2.8 **The hologram is a more appropriate model for your multifaceted brain than the camera***

To add still further to the extraordinary nature of this new development, if the plate is taken and smashed to smithereens with a hammer, each particle of the shattered plate will, when it is placed in front of the specially directed lasers, still produce the complete three-dimensional ghost.

The hologram thus becomes a far more reasonable model than the camera for the way in which your brain works. It begins to give us some idea of just how complex an organ it is that we carry about inside our heads.

Even this extremely refined piece of technology, however, falls far short of the unique capabilities of your brain. The hologram certainly approximates more closely the three-dimensional nature of your imagination, but its storage capacity is puny compared to the millions of images that your brain can randomly call up at an instant's notice. The hologram is also static, so it cannot perform any of the directional exercises of the kind described above that your brain finds so easy to do and yet must involve the most unimaginably intricate machinery. Even if a hologram were able to accomplish all this, it would not be able to do what your mind can – see its own self, with eyes closed, performing the operations!

IQ and your natural brilliance

Traditional IQ (intelligence quotient) tests, based on verbal and numerical reasoning, have been around for 100 years. Devised by a French theorist named Alfred Binet in the late nineteenth century, he proposed scales of intelligence that were originally designed to identify children with special needs. Supporters of traditional IQ tests believe that they measure our 'absolute intelligence'. Apart from the fact that an IQ score can be significantly changed by even a small amount of well-directed practice, however, there are other arguments against these tests being considered a means of measuring of 'absolute' IQ.

First, the Berkeley Study on Creativity showed that a person whose IQ assessment was high was not necessarily independent in thought, independent in action, either possessed of or able to value a good sense of humour, appreciative of beauty, reasonable, relativistic, able to enjoy complexity and novelty, original, comprehensively knowledgeable, fluent, flexible or astute.

Second, those who argue that IQ does measure a wide and absolute range of human abilities have failed to consider that the test should be concerned with three major areas: the brain being tested; the test itself; and the results. Unfortunately, the IQ protagonists have become too obsessed with the test and the results and have neglected the real nature of the brain being tested.

They have failed to realise that their tests do not test the full range of basic human abilities. Traditional IQ tests are based on the assumption that tests of verbal and mathematical skills are the truest markers for 'measuring' intelligence, when what they actually measure are untrained and undeveloped human performance. The protagonists' claims are much like those of an imaginary surveyor of women's feet sizes in the Orient at the time when their feet were restricted to make them small. From the crib, the babies' feet were placed in bandages until they were nearly full grown women. This was done to stunt their growth and produce 'dainty' feet.

To assume, however, as the surveyor might have done, that these measurements represent natural and fully developed bodily dimensions is as absurd as it is to assume that standard intelligence tests measure the natural dimensions of our minds. Our minds, like the women's feet, have been 'bound' by the way we have misjudged and mistrained them and are, therefore, not naturally developed.

In defence of IQ tests, it is interesting to note that they were *not* developed as a method, so often assumed, of 'suppressing the masses'. On the contrary, the French psychologist Alfred Binet observed that those children receiving higher education were almost exclusively from the upper classes. He considered this unfair and devised the first IQ tests in order to allow any child with developed mental abilities to qualify for ongoing studies. The tests gave unparalleled opportunities for children who would otherwise have been deprived of them.

It is best to consider IQ tests as games or 'markers' of a current stage of mental development in a few specified areas. They can then be used both to gauge present developments in those areas and as a basis from which those skills can be improved and developed and the IQ score raised appropriately.

The many-layered mind – your multiple intelligences

While tests on verbal, numerical and spatial reasoning are important contributors to overall intelligence, they do not account for other aspects of intelligent behaviour, such as creativity, interpersonal skills and skills in general knowledge. Let me give you just one striking example in the following case study.

What is smart? The Tony and Barry story

It all began when I was a boy of seven years old, commencing my first year of primary school in the seaside fishing village of Whitstable in Kent.

At that time, my best friend was a boy called Barry. Our prime interest at that age was in nature – in studying, collecting, breeding and protecting all forms of living things. Our homes were like small zoos!

As soon as the school day finished, Barry and I would rush out to the local fields, dykes and woods to pursue our passion.

Barry had an astonishing sensitivity to nature. He could distinguish – by their flight pattern as they flew towards the horizon – between the different butterflies and birds. He would be rattling off different species, while I was saying '... Er ... Cabbage White ... Sparrow ...', by which time they had all disappeared!

Early in the school year, we were informed by our teachers that we were being divided into different classes – 1a, 1b, 1c and 1d. We were told that it made no difference which class we were in. It took us a nanosecond to realise that 1a was for the 'bright boys' and the 'd' in 1d stood for 'dunce', 'dimwit', 'dullard', 'dumb' and 'disabled'.

I was put in 1a; my best friend, Barry, in 1d. We didn't talk or think about it much at all – that was just the way things were.

Within 1a we were subdivided even further. After being given our latest test result, we had to stand up and reorganise ourselves in descending order, from the top down, in terms of our latest ranking. The top scorer in the test sat in the back, right-hand seat, the second best scorer next to him and so on, snaking down to the front row where, in the front, right-hand seat, sat the boy with the lowest score in that test.

Where did little Tony Buzan sit?

Never in seat 1 and *never* in seat 2. Those seats were always 'reserved' for Mummery and Epps or Epps and Mummery! I was always somewhere below those pinnacles.

One day in 1a, our teacher was asking us some pretty tedious questions, such as 'Can you name two fish that you can find in English rivers?' (there are over a 100); 'What is the difference between an insect and a spider?' (there are over 15); 'What is the difference between a butterfly and a moth?' (again, there are over 15).

Some days later, our teacher, Mr Hake, proudly announced to the class, 'Someone has scored 100 per cent in a test!' Everybody, including me, looked at Mummery and Epps to see which one of them had done it again.

To our amazement, he called out 'Buzan!' I was stunned, because I *knew* that he had made a mistake – in every single test we had done, I knew that I had either left some questions blank or was certain that at least one of the answers I had written was wrong. There was no way that I could have scored a perfect mark.

We all had to move to our new seating positions all the same and, for the first time in my life, I found myself in the back, right-hand seat of 1a, waiting to be exposed! It was, however, a brief and pleasant experience to see, for the first time, the right profiles of Mummery and Epps!

Mr Hake handed out the papers and, to my amazement, the paper he put down in front of me had '100%', 'Top marks', 'Well done, boy, points for your team' *and* my name, in my writing, at the top of the page.

I scanned down the paper and quickly realised that it was the answers I had casually written down to the tedious questions on nature that Mr Hake had previously been asking us. My immediate reaction was, 'That wasn't a test – I could have given him 50 different fish, 15 differences between an insect and a spider and 15 more differences between a butterfly and a moth!' I was momentarily confused.

It slowly dawned on me that it *had* been a test and that when Mummery and Epps did well in tests, it was because they had the same relationship with their subject that I had with nature.

So I *was* number 1! It felt good ...

That feeling of achievement and euphoria lasted only briefly, but I realised something that was to paradigm shift my thinking and change my life. What was that realisation?

Sitting at the bottom of 'the snake' of excellence of over 100 pupils in the front row of 1d was my best friend Barry. Who knew more about nature – little Tony or little Barry?

Obviously little Barry.

In terms of excellence, Barry *should* have been sitting half a mile to the right of me in the top seat of 1a – he knew far more about the beauty and intricacy of nature than I did.

That realisation came as a deep shock because I now, out of the blue, had incontrovertible proof that the system I was in (the English education system) was not distinguishing 'intelligence' accurately. In this instance, it was actually judging the *best* to be the *worst*. The fact that my 'number 1' position had been achieved at the expense of my more brilliant 'dumb' friend made the realisation even more painful.

From that moment on, little Tony Buzan became an intellectual delinquent! I was always questioning, asking, 'Who says who's smart?' 'Who says who's *not* smart?' 'Who has the *right* to say who is smart and who is not smart?' 'What *is* smart?' 'What is *intelligence*?'

The rest of my life has been, and still is, spent in the pursuit of answers to those questions.

From the 1970s onwards, ideas about intelligence began to change as awareness of a number of other, *different* kinds of intelligence began to grow.

Along with the distinguished American psychologist Howard Gardner, I became aware of those different intelligences and how they worked in harmony with each of the others when they were properly developed. I was one of the original researchers and propagators of this alternative model of intelligence to that of the standard IQ.

The multiple intelligences include creative intelligence, personal intelligence, social intelligence, spiritual intelligence, physical intelligence and sensual intelligence, as well as the 'traditional' intelligences of numerical intelligence, spatial intelligence and verbal intelligence. For a full illustration of the multiple intelligences, see Figure 3.1 on page 33.

Each intelligence tends to have its own champions so that, for example, in social intelligence, Howard Gardner said that he considers it to be the most important because it is, in many instances, most highly correlated with general human success. Hans Eysenck, however, thought that the standard IQ was the most important. Leonardo da Vinci – although he did not call them 'intelligences' – said that the area of your skills that it is most important to develop is your sensual capacity – that is, your sensual intelligence.

The notion of multiple intelligences matches what we have already uncovered about the workings of the brain and the cortical skills (see Chapter 1). It is important to emphasise at the outset that these intelligences are *all* like muscles that can be trained and honed and *everyone* possesses the potential to develop every intelligence to a high degree.

The intelligences include:

- **verbal**: the development of 'word power' and the ability to juggle with the infinite manifestations of the alphabet

- **numerical**: the development of 'number power' and the ability to juggle with the infinite universe of numbers, as well as the ability to think logically

- **spatial**: the ability to negotiate three-dimensional space and handle objects in three dimensions.

These three intelligences constitute the bulk of the traditional IQ test. But to increase your own 'use of your head', you also need to make sure that you also develop the following equally important intelligences:

- **personal**: your self-awareness and ability to love yourself – to be your own best friend and best coach

- **social**: your ability to be successful in groups of one-to-one, one to small groups and one to large groups, as well as the ability to establish *enduring* relationships.

- **physical**: your general 'medical health' as well as your muscular strength, bodily flexibility and cardiovascular physical fitness

- **sensual**: your ability to use – as Leonard Da Vinci entreated us to – the multiple senses to the ultimate of their power and potential

- **creative**: the ability to think with the full range of your cortical skills and think abundantly, originally, imaginatively, flexibly, speedily and connectively

- **ethical/spiritual**: your compassion and love for other living things and the environment, charitability, understanding, 'big picture' thinking, positivity and generosity.

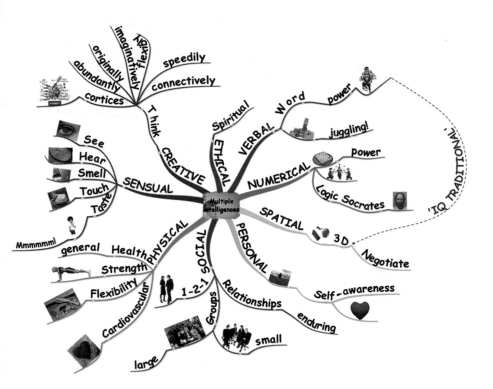

Figure 3.1 Mind Map of the multiple intelligences

Envisioning a world in which every human being is educated to develop these vast resources is the dream that educators and philosophers have had for millennia.

At the beginning of the twenty-first century, and at the beginning of the dawn of the age of intelligence, we have the opportunity to make this dream, finally, come true!

The human baby – a model of excellence

One of the most convincing cases for the excellence of the human brain is the functioning and development of the human baby. Far from being the 'helpless and incapable little thing' that many people assume it to be, it is the most extraordinary learning, remembering and intellectually advanced being. Even in its earliest stages, it surpasses the performance of the most sophisticated computers.

With very few exceptions, all babies learn to speak by the time they are two – many even earlier. Because this is so universal, it is taken for granted, but, if the process is examined more closely, you can see that it is extremely complex.

Try listening to someone speaking, while pretending that you have no knowledge of language and very little knowledge of the objects and ideas the language discusses. This task will be difficult and, because of the way sounds run into each other, the distinction between different words will often be totally unclear. Every baby who has learned to talk has overcome these difficulties and the difficulties of sorting out what makes sense and what doesn't. When babies are confronted with sounds like 'koooochiekooochiekoooo oooooaahhhhisn'thealovelyli'ldarling!' it is a wonder how they ever manage to make sense of us at all!

Young children's ability to learn language involves them in processes that include a subtle control of, and an inherent understanding of, rhythm, mathematics, music, physics, linguistics, spatial relationships, memory, integration, creativity, logical reasoning and thinking – the left and right cortex working from the word go.

You, who still doubt your own abilities, have yourself learned to talk and read. You should therefore find it difficult to attack that position when you yourself are evidence for the defence!

How our human brain has been 'reined in'

Even with the mounting evidence, a number of people still remain sceptical about the potential of human brains, pointing to the performance of most of us as contradicting that evidence. In response to this objection, a questionnaire was given to people from all areas of life to determine why this amazing organ is so underused. The questions are noted in the box opposite and, underneath each question, is noted the reply given by at least 95 per cent of the respondents. As you read, ask yourself the questions out loud.

By now, the answer to the original objection should be clear: the reasons our performances do not match even our minimum potentials is that we are given no information about what we are or how we can best utilise our inherent capacities.

1. In school were you taught anything about your brain and how understanding its functions could help you learn, memorise, think, etc.?

   No.

2. Were you taught anything about how your memory functions?

   No.

3. Were you taught anything about special and advanced memory techniques?

   No.

4. Anything about how your eye functions when you are learning and about how you can use this knowledge to your advantage?

   No.

5. Anything about the ranges of study techniques and how they can be applied to different disciplines?

   No.

6. Anything about the nature of concentration and how to maintain it when necessary?

   No.

7. Anything about motivation, how it affects your abilities and how you can use it to your advantage?

   No.

8. Anything about the nature of key words and key concepts and how they relate to note taking and imagination, etc.?

   No.

'Only human'!

Another survey I have carried out over the last 35 years and in 50 different countries asks people to imagine themselves in the following situation.

They have 'completed' an assignment and the results are totally and utterly disastrous. They attempt to avoid taking responsibility by giving such standard excuses for failure as, 'So and so didn't send me an e-mail on time', 'I had to go to the doctor just at the most crucial time in the project', 'It was their fault – if the information systems in this company had been better managed, everything would have been all right', 'My boss wouldn't let me do it in the way I suggested' and so on.

They are next asked to imagine that, despite all their brilliant excuse-making, they are finally cornered and have to admit that the whole catastrophe is indeed their responsibility.

Finally, they are asked to complete the 'admission of guilt' sentence that people commonly use: 'All right, all right, it was my fault, but what do you expect, I'm ...!'

In every group surveyed, in every country and in every language, the unanimous phrase used to complete the above sentence was '... only human!'

Humorous though this may initially seem, it reflects a worldwide and seriously misguided myth that we humans are somehow fundamentally inadequate and flawed and that is why we are responsible for the mounting catalogue of human 'mistakes' and 'failures'.

For another perspective on the scenario described above, consider these opposites.

You have done an astounding job and people are beginning to call you 'extraordinary, wonderful, amazing, a genius, brilliant' and describing your work as 'astounding, the best they have ever seen, unbelievable and unparalleled in its excellence'. For a little while, you go through the standard routines of denial, but, in the end, have to admit to your excellence.

How many times have you yourself or have you seen other people stand up proudly and pronounce, 'Yes! I am brilliant, I am a genius and the job that I have done is indeed amazing – so amazing it amazed even me! The reason for it is that I'm human!'

Probably never ...

Yet, it is this second scenario that is the more natural and, indeed, appropriate of the two. For human beings, you – as has been described in Chapter 1 – are indeed an extraordinary and, many would say, miraculous creation. Far from being an admission of failure, being 'only human' is an incredible statement! We have to learn how our brains operate in order to make the most of our extraordinary capabilities.

> The reason for our 'mistakes' and 'failures' is not that we are 'only human', but, at this very early stage in our evolution, we are still taking our first, babyish and tentative steps towards an understanding of the astounding biocomputer we each possess.

The reason, in our worldwide educational systems, we have spent so little time learning about how to learn is that we as a race have not known the fundamental principles of the operation of our super biocomputers.

To continue with the computer metaphor, we have not known about the software for the hardware of our brains.

In Part 2 of this, your 'operations manual for your brain', you'll find out how, what, why and when your brain recalls and learns information and how you can tap into mnemonics (memory devices) to double your memory capacity and release your true creativity.

If you **apply** these **(memory) principles** ... you will be able to **bestride** both **the world of memory** and **the world of knowledge** simultaneously, giving yourself the **advantages** that I found such training and application gave to me: greater **self-confidence**, a growing mastery of my **imagination**, improved **creativity**, vastly improved **perceptual skills** and, yes, a much **higher IQ!**

DOMINIC O'BRIEN, EIGHT TIMES WORLD MEMORY CHAMPION

Part 2

Harness your brain power

How are you at remembering facts and figures? Are you worried about recalling information under pressure in an exam? This part of the book provides you with vital insights into how you recall information and what makes things 'memorable'. Easy-to-follow mnemonics (memory techniques) and exercises are laid out to help you remember more, recall instantly and think better and more creatively.

Transform your ability to recall and learn information

This chapter explains and tests you on your innate ability to take in information, both *during* the time you are actually learning and *after* the period of learning has finished.

Recall during and after learning

One of the least understood or appreciated aspects of memory and learning is what you recall *during* and immediately *after* learning – that is, what you take in during a learning period and what you are able to recall after that learning ends. In fact, as you shall see from the tests and the discussion of the tests that follow in this chapter, an understanding of your 'understanding' and 'misunderstanding' is vital in priming you for optimum use of your fantastic memory facility. As you shall also see, 'memory' and 'understanding' do not work in the same way and, while you may understand *all* of what you are about to be tested on, you may not recall even *half* of it.

Don't assume either that, as you get older, your memory fades. That is false thinking. Also, do not believe that if you have moments when recalling information is a challenge, then you will never be able to hold anything in your mind for long ever again. That is more to do with not giving yourself time to pause and think and having poor methods of recall.

Your memory is, in fact, highly effective, but your process of recalling information may not be as effective as you'd like it to be. You need only to refine the way you access the information that is stored in your brain. To begin the process, try this simple exercise.

EXERCISE 1

Recall during *learning*

Here is a list of words. Read each word in the list once, quickly, in order. Read the complete list, one word after the other. To ensure that you do this properly, use a small card, covering each word as you read it. Unless you are a grand master of memory, you will not be able to remember all or even half of them, so simply try for as many as possible. Start now!

house	rope
floor	watch
wall	Shakespeare
glass	ring
roof	and
tree	of
sky	the
road	table
the	pen
of	flower
and	pain
of	dog
and	

Now cover the page and proceed to 'Responses and further questions' oppposite. Fill in as many of the words as you can for question 1. Go on to answer questions 2 to 6 as well.

Responses and further questions

When answering the questions, do not refer to the original list.

1 Fill in as many of the words, in order, as you can.

_____

_____

_____

_____

_____

_____

_____

_____

_____

_____

_____

_____

_____

_____

_____

_____

_____

2 How many of the words from the beginning of the list did you remember before making the first error?

3 Can you recall any words that appeared more than once in the list? If so, note them.

4 How many of the words within the last five did you remember?

5 Do you remember any item from the list that was outstandingly different from the rest?

6 How many words from the middle of the list can you remember that you have not already noted in answers to previous questions?

Recall during learning

Draw a line on the graph below that represents the amount you think your memory recalls *during* a learning period. The vertical left-hand line marks the *starting point* for the learning; the vertical right-hand line marks the point when learning *stops*; the bottom line represents *no* recall at all (complete forgetting); and the top line represents *perfect* recall.

Figures 4.1a–c show examples of graphs that have been filled in by three people, the lines representing the amount they felt *their* memories recalled *during* a learning period. The graphs start at 75 per cent because it is assumed that most standard learning does not produce 100 per cent understanding or recall.

There are, of course, many other alternatives so, when you have looked at these, complete the graph below to record the way you think *your* recall works.

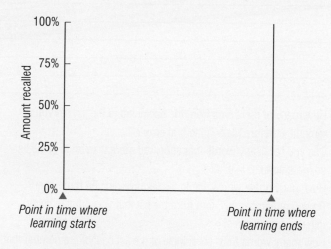

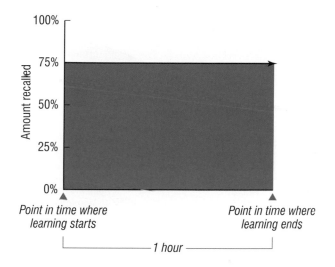

Figure 4.1a **A thought that his recall stayed constant during his learning**

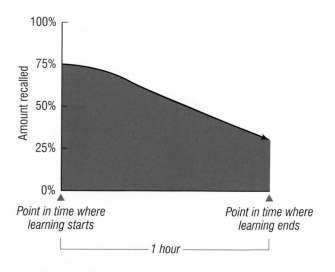

Figure 4.1b **B thought that she remembered more from the beginning of a learning period and less from the end**

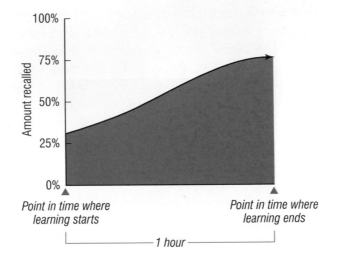

*Figure 4.1c **C** thought that he remembered less from the start and more from the end*

Feedback on the recall during learning exercises

In Exercise 1, almost everyone recalls similar information:

- one to seven words from the beginning of the list

- one or two words from the end of the list

- most of the words that appear more than once (in this case, 'the' and 'of')

- the outstanding word or phrase (in this case, 'Shakespeare')

- relatively few, if any, words from the middle of the list.

Why should such a similarity of results occur? This pattern shows that memory and understanding do not work in the same way – although all the words were *understood*, not all of them were *remembered*.

Our ability to recall information that we understand is related to several factors.

- We tend to remember 'first things' (known as the *primacy effect*) and last things (known as the *recency effect*) more easily than the 'things in between'. That is why we recall more information from the beginning and end of a learning period than the middle (see how the curve of the graph in Figure 4.2 begins high at the start, drops before the three peaks, then lifts again before the end). In the case of the word recall test, the words 'house' and 'dog' appear at the beginning *and* the end of the sequence, respectively.

- We learn more when things are *associated* or *linked* in some way, by using rhyme, repetition or something that connects with our senses (see points A, B, C in Figure 4.2). In the case of the word recall test, the repeated words include 'the', 'of' and 'and'; the associated words are 'tree' and 'flower' or 'house' and 'roof'.

- We also learn more when things are *outstanding* or *unique*. The name 'Shakespeare' stands out from the other words and sparks our imagination. This is known as the Von Restorff effect' (see point O in Figure 4.2).

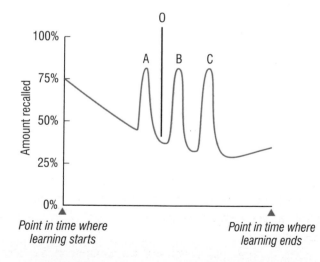

Figure 4.2 **Recall during learning. The graph shows that we recall more from the beginning and ends of a learning period than the middle. We also recall more when things are associated or linked (points A, B and C) and more when things are outstanding or unique (O) than when they're not**

This pattern of test scores shows very dramatically that memory and understanding do not work in exactly the same way as time progresses – all the words were understood; only some were recalled. The differences between the way in which memory and understanding function help explain why so many people find that they don't recall very much after hours of learning and understanding. The reason is that recall tends to get progressively worse as time goes on, unless the mind is given brief rests (see Figure 4.3).

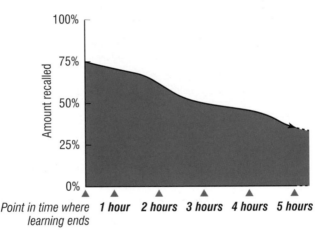

Figure 4.3 As time goes on, our recall of material being learned tends to get progressively worse, unless the mind is given proper rests

Thus, the graph you were asked to complete in Exercise 2 will be more complex in reality than the simple examples given in Figures 4.1a–c. Average scores from Exercise 1 produce a graph similar to Figure 4.2.

From the graph it is clear that, under normal circumstances and with understanding fairly constant:

● we tend to recall more at the beginning and ends of learning periods than the middle

● we tend to recall more of those items that are associated by repetition, sense, rhyming and so on than those which are not

- we tend to recall more things that are outstanding or unique (the psychologist who discovered this characteristic was Von Restorff, so such a memorisation event is known as the Von Restorff effect) than those which are not

- we tend to recall considerably less from the middle of learning periods.

If recall is going to be kept at a reasonable level, it is necessary to find the point at which recall and understanding work in greatest harmony. In normal study or work, this point occurs in a time period of between 20 and 50 minutes. A shorter period does not give the mind enough time to appreciate the rhythm and organisation of the material, while a longer period results in the continuing decline of the amount recalled (as shown in Figure 4.3).

If, then, a period of learning from a course seminar, book or the electronic media is to take two hours, it is far better to arrange brief breaks during those two hours. That way, the recall curve can be kept high, preventing it from dropping during the later stages of learning. Small breaks every half hour will guarantee eight relatively high points of recall, with four small drops in the middle. Each of the drops will be less than the main drop there would have been if there were no breaks during those two hours (see Figure 4.4).

Breaks are additionally useful as relaxation points. They get rid of the muscular and mental tension that inevitably build up during periods of concentration.

Taking breaks is important

Thus short, carefully spaced breaks are an important part of the learning and memory process. You will find it easier to recall information accurately when learning if you take breaks briefly and regularly – say, at 20- to 50-minute intervals – because they allow your mind time to absorb what has been learned. Importantly, when you take a break, you immediately create another 'recency' high point and, at the end of the break, you create another 'primacy' high point. Figure 4.4 shows three different patterns of recall for a two-hour period of learning.

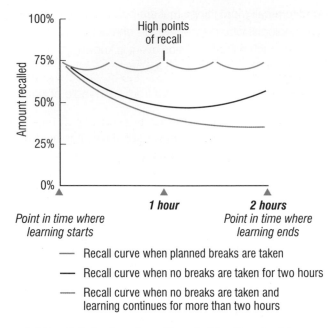

Figure 4.4 *Recall during learning, with and without breaks. A learning period of between 20 and 50 minutes produces the best relationship between understanding and recall*

- The top line shows the results when four short breaks were taken. The raised peaks show the moments when recall was highest. There are more high points on this line than any of the other memory curves because there are four 'beginnings and endings'. Also, the level of recall *remains* high.

- The middle line shows a recall curve for when no break was taken for two continuous hours. The beginning and end points show the highest level of recall, at 75 per cent, but, overall, the retention level dropped to below that figure.

- The bottom line shows what happened when no break was taken and study continued for more than two hours. This approach is obviously counter-productive as the recall line never picked up – in fact it kept falling downwards, below the 50 per cent mark.

The lesson here is that, without rests, your recall goes steadily downhill.

- The more well-spaced, short breaks you have, the more beginnings and endings you have, the better your brain will be able to remember.

- Brief breaks are also essential for relaxation as they relieve the muscular and mental tension that inevitably builds up during periods of intense concentration.

EXERCISE 3

Recall after learning

The blank graph below is for you to record the way your memory behaves *after* a learning period has been completed. The vertical left-hand line marks the *end point* of your learning; there is no right-hand vertical line because it is assumed that the 'afterwards' could be a few years; the bottom line represents *no* recall at all; and the top line represents *perfect* recall.

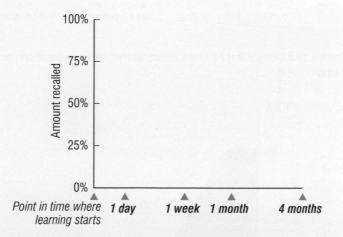

As with Exercise 2, there are many alternatives, so complete the graph in the way that most closely represents how *your* recall *after* a learning period behaves. For the purpose of the exercise, you can assume that nothing happens after your learning period to remind you of the information you learned.

Feedback on the recall after learning exercise

In Exercise 3 you were asked to fill in a graph, this time indicating the way in which you thought your recall functioned after a period of learning had been completed. The examples given in Figures 4.5a–c are the kinds of answers many people have given when completing the exercise, although there has been a much wider variety of responses overall.

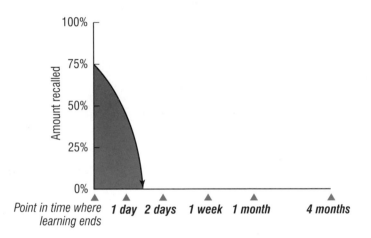

*Figure 4.5a **A thought that he forgot nearly everything in a very short period of time***

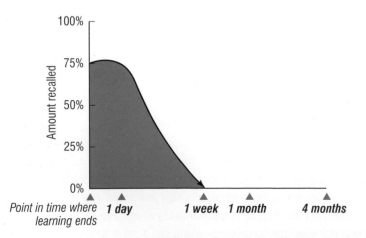

*Figure 4.5a **B thought that her recall was constant for a little while, then it dropped off fairly steeply***

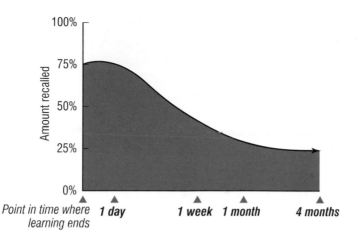

*Figure 4.5c **C** thought that his memory stayed constant for a while, then dropped off slowly, levelling out at a certain point*

Apart from those shown above, other answers included straight lines plunging almost immediately to nothing; variations on the more rapid drop – some falling to 0 per cent, others always maintaining a level above zero, however small; variations on the slower tailing off, also with some falling to 0 per cent and others above that; and variations on these themes, showing rises and falls of varying degree (see Figure 4.6).

The surprising truth of the matter is that none of the examples shown earlier, nor any of the estimates shown, is correct. They have all neglected a particularly significant factor: recall after a learning period initially *rises* and only *then* declines, following a steeply falling concave curve that levels off (see Figure 4.7).

Once it is realised that this brief rise *does* take place, the reason for it can be understood. At the very moment when a learning period is finished, your brain has not had enough time to integrate the new information it has assimilated, especially the last items. It needs a few minutes to complete and link firmly all the interconnections within the new material – to let it 'sink in'.

The decline that takes place after the small rise is a steep one – within 24 hours of an hour-long learning period, at least 80 per cent of the detailed information learned is lost. This enormous drop must be prevented, and can be by means of proper review.

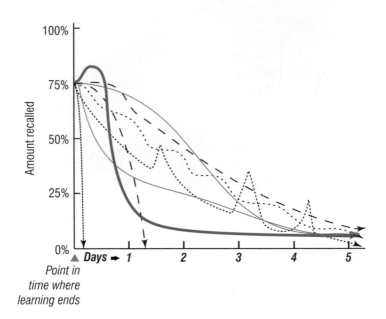

*Figure 4.6 **The graph shows the different kinds of answers people gave when they were asked to show how their recall functioned after a one-hour period of learning. The blue lines signify the most commonly assumed declines in recall. The red line shows the** actual **pattern measured by psychological studies: notice the initial rise before the steep fall***

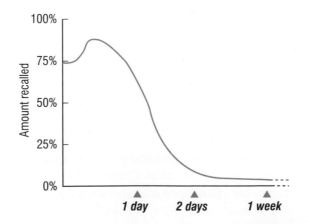

*Figure 4.7 **Human recall rises for a short while after learning and then falls steeply (80 per cent of the details are forgotten within 24 hours)***

Memory – review techniques and theory

If a review is organised properly, what happened in the graph in Figure 4.7 can be changed, keeping the level of recall at the high point reached shortly after learning has been completed. In order to accomplish this, a programmed pattern of review must take place, each review being done at the time just before recall is about to drop.

For example, the first review should take place about ten minutes after an hour-long learning period and should itself take five minutes. That will keep the level of recall high for approximately one day, when the next review should take place, this time for a period of two to four minutes. After then, recall will probably be retained for approximately a week, when another two-minute review can be completed, followed by a further review after about a month. After this time, the knowledge will be lodged in your long-term memory. That means it will be familiar to you in the way that your telephone number is familiar, needing only the most occasional nudge to maintain it (see Figure 4.8).

The first review, especially if notes have been taken, should be a fairly complete, note-making form of revision, which may mean scrapping your original notes and substituting revised and final copy for them.

The second, third and fourth review sessions should take the following form. Without referring to final notes, jot down or Mind Map on a piece of paper everything that you can recall. Check what you have written against your final notes and make any corrections or additions to what you recalled. Both notes and jottings should be in the form of Mind Maps (which are explained in Part 3).

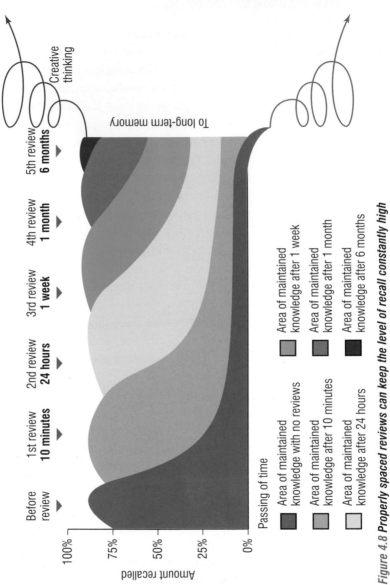

*Figure 4.8 **Properly spaced reviews can keep the level of recall constantly high***

Recall after learning – the value of repetition

New information is stored first in your short-term memory. To transfer information to your long-term memory takes rehearsal and practice.

On average, you will need to repeat an action at least five times before the information is transferred permanently to your long-term memory, which means that you need to revisit what you have learned using one or more memory techniques on a regular basis.

This neatly condenses into your memory formula (the arrow signifies 'into'):

$$STM \rightarrow LTM = 5R$$

This formula stands for 'from short-term memory to long-term memory requires five repetitions/reviews/recalls'.

My recommendation is to review and repeat what you have learned these five times as follows:

1 shortly after you have learned it

2 one day after you have learned it

3 one week after you first learned it

4 one month after you first learned it

5 three to six months after you first learned it.

Each time you review and recall, you are revisiting the information that you have learned and will also be adding to your knowledge. Your creative imagination has a part to play in long-term memory and, the more you go over information that you have learned, the more you will link it to other information and knowledge you have already retained.

The more we learn, the more we remember. The more we remember, the more we learn.

The advantages of reviewing v. the disadvantages of not reviewing

One of the most significant aspects of proper reviews is the cumulative effect it has on all aspects of learning, thinking and remembering. If you do not review, you will be continually wasting the effort you put in to any learning task, as well as putting yourself at a serious disadvantage.

Each time you approach a new learning situation, your recall of previous knowledge gained will be at a very low ebb and the connections that should be made automatically will be dismissed. That will mean your understanding of the new material will not be as complete as it could be and the efficiency and speed with which you work through the new material will also be reduced. Where such a negative process is repeated and repeated, it results in a downward spiral that ends in a feeling of general despair of ever being able to learn anything. Each time new material is learned, it is forgotten and each time new material is approached, it is with a heavy heart. The result is that many people, after having finished their formal exams, seldom, if ever, approach textbooks again.

Failure to review is just as bad for general memory. If each new piece of information is neglected, it will not remain in our memories at a conscious level, so will not be available to form new memory connections. As memory is a process that is based on linking and association, the fewer items there are in our 'recall store', the less will be the possibility for new items to be registered and connected.

On the opposite side of this coin, the advantages of reviewing are enormous. The more you maintain your current body of knowledge, the more you will be able to absorb and handle. When you study, the expanding amount of knowledge at your command will enable you to digest new knowledge far more easily, each new piece of information being absorbed into the context of your existing store of relevant information (see Figure 4.8). The process is much like that of making a snowball by rolling a small ball along the ground: it gets rapidly bigger the more it rolls and, eventually, it continues to roll under its own momentum. Good review habits will have a snowball effect, enhancing your confidence, your work and your life.

Master mnemonics to double your memory and more

Mnemonics (pronounced 'nem-*on*-ics') is the name given to memory aids that help you to remember something. It may be a word, picture, system or other device that will help you to recall a phrase, name or sequence of facts. The 'm' in mnemonic is silent and the word comes from the Greek word *mnemon*, which means 'mindful'. It is also based on the name of the Greek goddess of memory, Mnemosyne.

The principles for perfect memory laid down by the Greeks fit in exactly with the information we now know about the left and right hemispheres of the brain (see page 16). Without a physiological or scientific basis, the Greeks realised that, in order to remember well, you have to use every aspect of your mind.

Since the time of the Greeks, certain individuals have impressed the rest of us with the most amazing feats of memory. They have been able to remember hundreds of items, backwards and forwards and in any order, dates and numbers, names and faces and have been able to perform special memory feats, such as memorising whole areas of knowledge perfectly or remembering decks of cards in the order anyone chooses to present them.

Most of us will have used mnemonic techniques to learn things during our schooldays, even if we didn't realise it at the time. How about 'i before e except after c' for grammar and spelling or the phrase 'Every Good Boy Deserves Favour' to help remember the notes on the treble clef (from the lowest), EGBDF.

If the initial letters used in a mnemonic form a word, it is known as an *acronym* (ac-ro-nim). An acronym is a word that is formed from the first letters of each word, such as UNESCO, which stands for the United Nations Educational, Scientific and Cultural Organization.

Many of us will have learned the poem 'Thirty days hath September, April, June and November …' to help remember which months have 30 days and which have 31 ('except for February, alone …'). That too is a mnemonic – a device to help you remember.

Mnemonics work by stimulating your imagination and using words and other tools to encourage your brain to make associations.

Why memory training is good for you

Experiments with mnemonic techniques have shown that if a person scores 9 out of 10 when using such a technique, that same person will score 900 out of 1000, 9000 out of 10,000 and 900,000 out of 1,000,000. Similarly, someone who scores perfectly out of 10 will score perfectly out of 1,000,000. These results indicate yet again the apparently infinite capacity of the brain to store and create information.

Traditionally, these techniques have been scorned as mere tricks, but attitudes towards them have changed. It has been realised that the methods which initially enable minds to remember something more easily and quickly, then remember it for much longer afterwards, are actually using the brain's natural abilities.

Current knowledge about the ways in which our minds work shows that mnemonic principles are indeed closely connected to the basic ways in which our brains function. The use of mnemonic principles has consequently gained respectability and popularity, and they are currently being taught in universities and schools as additional aids in the general learning process. The improvement in memory that can be achieved is quite remarkable and the range of techniques that can be used is wide.

World Memory Championships

At the beginning of the 1990s, I established The Memoriad, the World Memory Championships. Today, as a result of these championships, staggering feats of memory are being achieved, previous psychological limits are being smashed, the boundaries of what is possible are being extended and amazing new records established. For example, Dominic O'Brien, the first and eight times World Memory Champion, was able to memorise a complete pack of cards in 42.6 seconds, as well as memorising a randomly generated 100-digit binary number in 57 seconds! In the 2007 UK Memory Championships, Ben Pridmore memorised a single shuffled deck of playing cards in 26.28 seconds, beating the previous world record of 31.16 seconds set by Andi Bell and breaking the magic 30 second barrier – the mind sport equivalent of the 4-minute mile (see page 200 for more on the World Memory Championships).

The core memory principles

Imagination and *association* are the foundation stones on which memory techniques are based. The more effectively you can use them – by means of key memory devices such as words, numbers and images – the more supercharged and effective your mind and memory will be.

To remember well, and spark off your associated and linked mental landscape, I have devised the following 12 memory techniques, which can be remembered by keeping in mind the mnemonic of the initial letters of each of the techniques – SMASHIN SCOPE (see Figure 5.1). Imagination and association are core values of the following SMASHIN SCOPE mnemonic technique.

Figure 5.1 **Mind Map for SMASHIN SCOPE**

1 Senses/sensuality

The more you can visualise, hear, taste, smell, feel or sense the thing that you are trying to recall, the better you will reinforce your ability to remember and be able to call to mind the information when you need it. Everything you experience, everything you learn and everything you enjoy is delivered to your brain via your senses – that is, vision, hearing, smell, taste, touch and spatial awareness of your body and its movement (known as kinaesthesia).

The more sensitive you become to the information that your senses receive, the better you will be able to remember. The great 'natural' memorisers, and the great mnemonists, develop exceptional sensitivity in each of their senses, then blend these senses to produce enhanced recall. The blending of the senses is known as *synaesthesia*.

2 Movement

In any mnemonic image, movement adds another giant range of possibilities for your brain to 'link in' and thus remember. As your images move, make them three-dimensional. As a subdivision of movement, use rhythm in your memory images. The more rhythm and variation of rhythm in your mental pictures, the more they will be outstanding and thus the more they will be remembered.

3 Association

Whatever you wish to memorise, make sure that you associate or link it to something stable in your mental environment, such as the peg system: one = bun. If you ground your images in reality by associating them with something that is familiar, it will anchor them in a location and you will then be able to remember the information more easily. Association works by linking or pegging information to other information, such as the use of numbers, symbols and order and patterns (see Figure 5.2).

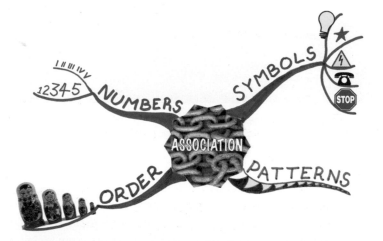

Figure 5.2 *Mini Mind Map showing different ways of using association to enhance memory*

4 Sexuality

We all have a virtually perfect memory in this area. Use it!

5 Humour

Have fun with your memory. The funnier, more ridiculous, absurd and surreal you make your images, the more outstandingly memorable they will be. One of the surrealist painter Salvador Dali's most famous works is entitled *The Persistence of Memory* (see Figure 5.3).

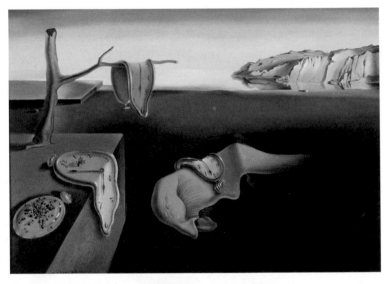

Figure 5.3 The Persistence of Memory
Source: © Salvador Dalí, Fundació Gala-Salvador Dalí, DACS, 2010 and Bettman/CORBIS

6 Imagination

Einstein said, 'Imagination is more important than knowledge. For knowledge is limited, whereas imagination embraces the entire world, stimulating progress, giving birth to evolution.' Your imagination has no limits; it is boundless and it stimulates your senses and, therefore, your brain (see Figure 5.4). Having an unlimited imagination makes you open to new experiences and less inclined to hold yourself back from learning new things.

Harness your brain power

*Figure 5.4 **Mini Mind Map showing different ways in which you can use your imagination to help you remember***

7 Number

Numbers have a powerful impact on your memory because they bring order to your thoughts. Numbers help to make memories more specific.

8 Symbolism

Symbols are a compact and coded way of using imagination and exaggeration to anchor memory. Creating a symbol to prompt a memory is rather like creating a logo. It tells a story and connects to, and is representative of, something larger than the image itself. You may also use traditional symbols, such as a stop sign or light bulb.

9 Colour

Where appropriate, and whenever possible, use *all* the colours of the rainbow to make your ideas more 'colourful' and therefore more memorable. Use colour in your imaginings, drawings and notes so that your visual sense is heightened and your brain is stimulated to enjoy the experience of seeing.

10 Order and/or sequence

In combination with the other principles, order and/or sequence allow for much more immediate referencing and increase your brain's possibilities for 'random access'. Examples include little to big, colour grouping, sorting by category and hierarchical aggregation.

11 Positivity

In most instances, positive and pleasant images are better for memory purposes than negative ones because they make your brain *want* to *return* to the images (see Figure 5.5). Certain negative images, even when all the principles above are applied and though, in and of themselves, they are 'memorable', could be blocked by the brain because it finds the prospect of returning to such images unpleasant.

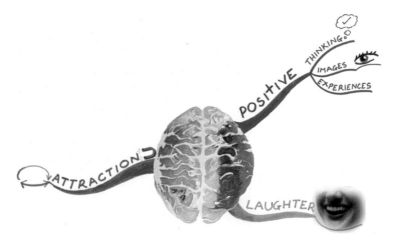

*Figure 5.5 **Mini Mind Map showing how you can use positive thinking to aid your memory***

12 Exaggeration

In all your images, exaggerate size, shape and sound. Think large and be absurd in your imaginings. The more exaggerated your images are, in size, shape and sound, the better you will be able to remember them. Think of children's favourite characters. The cartoon ogre Shrek and the giant Hagrid in the Harry Potter stories, for example, are larger than life and stay alive in the mind's eye more readily than other characters in the films.

Where do we go from here?

As we discovered earlier, for your brain to work effectively, you need to use *both* sides of it. It can be no coincidence that the two foundation stones of memory coincide with the two main activities of your brain:

Imagination

Association

} *Together they = MEMORY*

Your memory gives you your sense of who you are, so it is appropriate that the mnemonic to remember the above is:

I AM

As you will discover later, it is these two fundamental brain principles – *imagination* and *association* – that form the basis of Mind Mapping.

It is interesting to note that the principles laid out in the mnemonic acronym SMASHIN SCOPE outlined above also form the core structure of Mind Maps and it was my exploration of memory principles that led me to develop the Mind Map initially as a mnemonic device (see Part 3).

Now that I have explained the basic theory behind memory systems, I shall introduce you to a simple system for remembering up to ten items. First, you need to try this simple test.

EXERCISE 4

Simple memory systems and mnemonics

Here is a list of ten words next to ten numbers. As with Exercise 1, read each line once, covering the ones read with a card as you progress down the list. The purpose of this is to remember which words go with which number.

4	leaf	5	student
9	shirt	8	pencil
1	table	3	cat
6	orange	7	car
10	poker	2	feather

Now turn the page and write down the words in the order requested.

Here are the numbers 1 to 10. From memory, fill in next to each number the word that originally appeared next to it. The numbers are not listed in the same order as before. Only refer back to the original list after you have filled in as many as you can, then write down how many you get right.

1	_____	7	_____
5	_____	4	_____
3	_____	6	_____
8	_____	10	_____
9	_____	2	_____

Score: _____

Now let's look at some special memory systems for memorising this ten-word list.

The number–rhyme memory system

Here are the ten items again, set out in numerical order.

1 table	6 orange
2 feather	7 car
3 cat	8 pencil
4 leaf	9 shirt
5 student	10 poker

In order to remember them, it is necessary to have some system that enables us to use the *associative* and *linking* power of your memory to connect them with their proper numbers.

One of the best and easiest systems for this is the *number–rhyme* system, in which each number has a rhyming word connected to it. Easy to learn, this mnemonic is ideal when you need to remember short lists of items for a brief period of time.

The following list of rhyming words will start you off. You can see that each number has a corresponding word that rhymes with it.

1 bun	6 sticks
2 shoe	7 heaven
3 tree	8 skate
4 door	9 vine
5 hive	10 hen

In order to remember the first list of arbitrary words used in Exercise 4, it is necessary to link them in some strong manner with the rhyming words connected to the numbers given above. If this is done successfully, the answer to a question such as, 'What word was connected to number 5?' will be easy. The rhyming word for 5, 'hive', will be recalled automatically and with it will come the connected image of the word that has to be remembered – in this case, 'student'. This is what you need to do.

- Use your imagination and, if you wish, different images, to come up with alternative, memorable images/rhymes that work for you.

- Choose words that are easy for you to remember and associate with each number, then draw your images in the boxes on the next page, using as much colour and imagination as possible.

- To help you create the clearest mental picture possible for each image, close your eyes and imagine it projected on to the insides of your eyelids or, if you prefer, a screen inside your head.

- Hear, feel, smell or experience the image that works best for you, in the way that works best for you. For example, think of what you ate for lunch yesterday. How does your brain recreate it for you?

When you have completed that task, close your eyes and run through the numbers from one to ten to ensure that you have remembered each of your rhyming image associations. Then count backwards from ten to one, doing the same thing.

The faster you are able to do this, the better your memory will become. The more you practise the technique, the more your associative and creative thinking abilities will improve.

Practise recalling numbers at random until the numbers, rhymes and images associated with them become second nature.

1	6
2	7
3	8
4	9
5	10

Harness your brain power

The number–rhyme system in action

Once you have memorised your number–rhyme key words and images, you will then be ready to put the number–rhyme system into action.

Take the list on page 68 and link it to the rhyming words given on page 69. Refer back and you will see that the number–rhyme pairings could possibly become perhaps the following images (see Figure 5.6 on page 73).

1 **bun** + table

Imagine a giant bun on top of a fragile table, in the process of crumbling under the weight. Smell the freshly baked aroma of your favourite bun, and imagine its taste.

2 **shoe** + feather

Imagine your favourite shoe with an enormous feather growing out of the inside, preventing you from putting your shoe on, and feel it tickling your feet.

3 **tree** + cat

Imagine a large tree with either your own cat or a cat you know stuck in the very top branches, frantically scrambling about and mewing loudly.

4 **door** + leaf

Imagine that your bedroom door is a giant leaf, crunching and rustling as you open it.

5 **hive** + student

Imagine a student at her desk, dressed in black and yellow stripes, buzzing busily in a hive of activity or honey dripping on her pages.

6 **sticks** + orange

Imagine large sticks puncturing the juicy surface of an orange that is as big as a beach ball. Feel and smell the juice of the orange squirting out.

7 **heaven** + car

Imagine all the angels in heaven sitting on cars rather than clouds. Experience yourself driving the car that you consider to be heavenly.

8 skate + pencil

Imagine yourself skating on the pavement, hearing the sound of the wheels on the ground and seeing the multicoloured pencils attached to your skates, creating fantastic coloured shapes wherever you go.

9 vine + shirt

Imagine a vine as large as Jack and the Beanstalk's beanstalk and, instead of leaves on the vine, picture brightly coloured shirts hanging all over it, blowing in the breeze.

10 hen + poker

Now it's your turn ... Imagine a hen, with a poker ...

The key words above are in bold. These are your memory triggers and remain consistent, no matter what else you are trying to remember. In order to remember the list from Exercise 4, it is necessary to link them in some strong manner with the rhyming words connected with the numbers. If that is done successfully, the answer to a question such as, 'What word is connected with number 5?' will be easy. The rhyming word for 5, 'hive', will be recalled automatically, then with it will come the connected image of the word that has to be remembered – in this case, 'student'.

Check that all the word and image associations are *strong*, *positive*, *simple* and *clear* and make sure they are working for you. You can be sure that, each time you practise, your technique will improve and your memory will perform increasingly at an above-average level.

Use *imagination* and *association* to create links between the pairs of words.

It is when you start to create your own sequences that you will feel this technique working. You don't have to use the examples given here; create your own. The more absurd, surreal, over-the-top and sensual you are able to make your associations, the better you will tap into your own imagination. The more you practise, the easier the technique will be and, eventually, it will become totally natural for you.

Such a key memory system will give a supercharged boost to your recall and remembering powers.

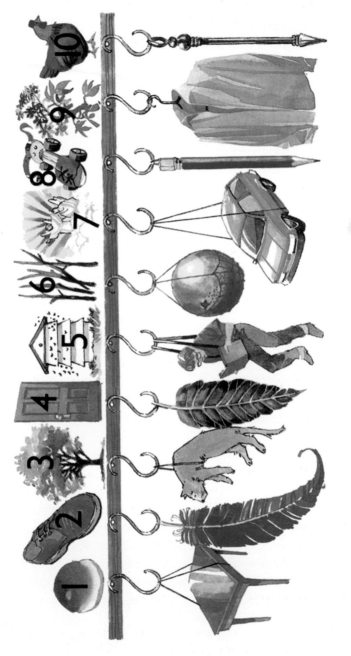

Figure 5.6 The number-rhyme memory system

Number–rhyme system review

As a final review of this system, check your improving memory once again.

In the spaces given below, write the rhyming key words for the number–rhyme system and, next to them, the words in the list used in Exercise 4.

Rhyming key words   **Word connected**

1 _____   _____
2 _____   _____
3 _____   _____
4 _____   _____
5 _____   _____
6 _____   _____
7 _____   _____
8 _____   _____
9 _____   _____
10 _____   _____

With a little practice, it is possible to remember ten out of ten each time, even using the same system. The words to be remembered can, like clothes, be taken off the hook and other clothes, substituted. The only words that must remain constant – and, in any case, are almost impossible to forget – are the rhyming key words.

There are many other memory systems, too, including the *major* system, which enables recall of more than a thousand items in the manner of the number–rhyme system, as well as giving a key for memorising numbers and dates, and the *face–name* system, which helps prevent the embarrassing and widespread failure to recall either the names or faces of people we have met. Another system, the *number–shape* system, uses associated shapes as memory triggers for the numbers one to ten instead of the rhyming words. For further information on all these systems, see *The Memory Book* (BBC Active, 2010).

As you will have gathered throughout the course of this chapter, memory is primarily an associative and linking process that depends in large part on Key Words and key concepts properly imagined. These memory/mnemonic techniques really do work – sometimes so well as to be considered by some unbelievable. I give you this case study to prove the point.

The 'impossible task'

A class of 14-year-old students in Sweden were set, by their teacher, what he described as 'an impossible task'. He stated that they should simply try to do as well as they could. The students were, in one evening, to memorise as many of the countries and capitals of the world as they could. This was part of their studies of general subjects, which included history and geography.

One of the children was a young boy called Lars Sundberg who was an average-to-good student and not totally focused on his academic pursuits because he was a first-class junior tennis player.

Lars went home, particularly depressed by what he considered to be an onerous task and told his father, Tomas (who was a director of the Salen Shipping Group, one of the major shipping companies in Sweden), that he thought it was an unfair and, indeed, impossible assignment.

Lars' father had brought in brain training to the company and had invited Tony Buzan to lecture on the contents of *Use Your Head* to the entire company. He had also established within the company a 'Brain Room' where any member of the organisation could go to either rest and think or Mind Map or brainstorm or carry out any function connected with thinking, learning and memory.

Tomas had been particularly impressed by the increased capacity he had personally experienced in his own memory since using what he had learned from the lecture and had even 'used his head' to impress the company's clients about Salen's shipping portfolio and offerings for the customer. All this took place in Sweden's capital city of Stockholm, where Salen's headquarters are located.

Tomas enthusiastically set about teaching his son how to apply memory techniques to what was, in reality, not that difficult at all. The way in which they memorised all the cities was to use the peg system in conjunction with the link system, relying on the number–rhyme, number–shape and alphabet systems, as well as part of the major system (see *The Memory Book*, BBC Active, 2010).

Father and son, as a result, were able to remember the cities, their countries and, in virtually all instances, their proper pronounciation.

Lars' brain was filled with wonderful and colourful images and associations that were connected to the maps of the countries themselves. So, while he was memorising, he was seeing the city connected to its memory key image word in the system, as well as simultaneously placing the city in its correct geographical location in its own country. On top of learning the capital cities, the boy also acquired a tremendously extended knowledge of where *all* the countries in the world were. This was striking as, previously, he had been confused about countries not local to Scandinavia!

Two weeks later, Tomas was phoned by the headteacher of his son's school. He apologised for having to convey the bad news that his son had been cheating. The headteacher explained that, in a recent geography test, the top mark in the school had been 123, and that his son had scored over 300, 'proving' that he had cheated!

The story ended happily, however, with Lars teaching his schoolmates how to use their memories as his father had taught him.

You now understand the nature of recall *during* learning and recall *after* learning. You have also practised the essential and easy-to-follow mnemonic techniques in this chapter to help you remember, fire up your imagination and encourage your brain to make associations.

In the next chapter, you will learn how to apply these stimulants to boost your creativity, too.

Harness your brain power

Energy 'plus' and 'into' memory yields infinite creativity:
$E \twoheadrightarrow M = C^{\infty}$

Memory and creativity have historically tended to be categorised as separate cognitive skills. In my researches over the past 40 years into the mind, memory and creativity, however, I have constantly found the two to be inseparable and developed a formula (see Figure 6.1) that demonstrates the intimate relationship between your memory and creativity.

*Figure 6.1 **The memory and creativity formula***

Can you work out what the symbols stand for?

Both *memory* and *creativity* are based on *imagination* and *association*. Thus, putting effort into developing your memory will simultaneously develop your creativity and vice versa. Therefore, the formula decodes to:

Energy + and into memory yields infinite creativity

Whenever you are practising or applying mnemonic techniques, you are at the same time practising and enhancing your powers of creativity.

What drives your creativity?

Creativity is the development of original ideas, images and solutions based on existing old ideas by using imagination and association. The driving force behind your creativity is your imagination.

Creativity involves going on imaginative journeys, and taking your brain into original and previously unexplored realms. These new associations give rise to the new realisations that the world calls 'creative breakthroughs'.

It becomes clear that memory is the use of imagination and association to hold the past in its appropriate place and recreate the past in the present, whereas creativity is the use of imagination and association to plant the present thought in the future and recreate in reality the present thought in some future time.

Working creatively produces multiple ideas, which can then be fully assessed and analysed, with the very best of these innovations being processed and turned into 'solutions' and reality. That is where you can reap the rewards of such creativity in creative behaviours and increasing your valuable 'intellectual capital'.

It was the great genius Leonardo da Vinci (see Figure 6.2) who proposed that to be truly creative you need to:

- develop your senses

- study the art of science

- study the science of art

- realise that everything, in some way, connects to everything else.

Figure 6.2 **Self-portrait of Leonardo da Vinci**
Source: © Getty Images/Stuart Gregory

Dedication and energy are then needed to embed this new way of thinking into how you think, study, learn and memorise.

Creativity can – and should – be applied in all areas of learning. Being creative can be difficult when you are obliged to work within codes of conduct and rules and regulations that seem to deaden all levels of thinking. That is precisely when you need to look for fresh perspectives and, even if you feel anxious, it will soon become exciting and liberating.

How can you achieve this? By applying techniques that, once they become second nature, will support you in all your endeavours.

Creative intelligence

This test taps into the more radiant and explosive of your thought processes, which will lead you into new realms of thinking and expression.

To score this test, give yourself 0 if the statement is absolutely untrue of you and 10 if it's explosively true.

1   I enjoy drawing, painting, sculpting and using 3D perspective.   *Score:* _____

2   I enjoy dancing to different beats and listening to all different forms of music.   *Score:* _____

3   I enjoy creative writing, poetry and storytelling.   *Score:* _____

4   I enjoy the theatre and acting, including comedy, tragedy, mime and playing the fool.   *Score:* _____

5   I enjoy humour and making people laugh.   *Score:* _____

6   People often say that I'm crazy, unpredictable, a 'one-off' (in a nice way).   *Score:* _____

7   I regularly attend the theatre, art exhibitions, concerts and other cultural events.   *Score:* _____

8   I have a rich and varied dream world.   *Score:* _____

9   I consider myself an exceptionally creative and productive individual.   *Score:* _____

10   I love to daydream and am a good creative daydreamer.   *Score:* _____

Score chart
Statement number

1	2	3	4	5	6	7	8	9	10	Total

Analysis
A score of 50 or more indicates that you are doing very well. A score of 100 means that you are a genius when it comes to creativity! Test yourself again from time to time to watch your score rise.

Creative intelligence

For this test, which is based on work on creative thinking by American psychologist E. Paul Torrence, you need a pen, paper and a watch.

First, think of an elastic band ... (see Figure 6.3) Now write down – in 60 seconds, on a piece of paper – all the uses you can possibly think of for an elastic band. Now check your score.

0–5	5–7	7–8	8–9	9–12	13+
Your brain is better than you think. Revisit earlier chapters and use your imagination to the full	Average – your creativity training has been either weak, small or misdirected. Revisit the previous two chapters on memory	Well done! This is above average. Read on and get the most from *Use Your Head*	Exceptionally good creativity score! Another go and it wouldn't take much for you to get into genius category	You are a creative master, verging on achieving international fame!	Genius level! The accolades will keep on coming. A Pulitzer Prize awaits, even a Nobel Prize!! This type of intelligence improves with age

How many uses did you come up with? The normal brain will produce from 0 to 8 ideas – 3 or 4 being average – while 9 to 12 is to good, 13 to 15 excellent and a score of 16 or more equivalent, in creativity terms, to an IQ score of above 200.

Figure 6.3 **What could you do with these?**
Source: POD/Photodisc. Photograph by Steve Cole

Creative intelligence

Now write down on the flip side of paper all the *non* uses for an elastic band that you can possibly think of (that is, things you couldn't even remotely think of doing with it) – again, in 60 seconds. Be as imaginative as you like.

What the exercises tell us

The message from the elastic band test is that, on average, people score higher for Exercise 8 – the *negative* test – than for Exercise 7. The reason for that is, in our mental landscapes, the number of possible *non* uses for something is infinite, whereas the number of *actual* uses is a very small number.

Having thought of and noted the non-uses, try to see if there is any way in which you *could* make any of them into a use.

What people find when they begin this transitional exercise is that, as they progress, *every* one of their non-uses becomes a possible use. As the thinking progresses, their infinite universe of non-uses gradually shrinks and shrivels until it reaches zero. In other words, there are no non-uses for an elastic band – or, indeed, for *anything* – because the brain, when it is creatively fired and using its energies and tools appropriately, can find an infinite number of uses for anything, and therefore an *infinite infinity* of uses. As the negative universe shrinks to zero, the positive universe, which originally was a tiny number, swells and expands to become *infinite*.

What we have been doing, theoretically, is putting the infinity symbol – ∞ – in a place that is exactly opposite the place it should reside. That is confirmed by and confirms Leonardo da Vinci's creative statement – 'everything, in some way, connects to everything else.' It also completely shifts the world's perspectives on problems and solutions. On average, people assume that there are theoretically infinite insoluble problems and only a relatively minor number of solutions. The fact is, *every* problem has a solution and there are no insoluble problems for a human brain that is properly trained, activated and aware of its creative functions. That leaves us in a world where everything is hopeful rather than being fundamentally depressing and without hope.

It is also important to state here that we have in the past thought of the brain as a problem-solving mechanism. That is in *part* true, but we have erroneously put the emphasis on the wrong place. The brain is, primarily, a *solution-finding* mechanism.

If you consider yourself a problem-solving human being, your focus will be on problems. If you consider yourself a *solution-finding* human being, your focus will be on solutions. Take your pick!

The creative brain

Where are you physically located when you come up with your great bursts of creative ideas? Your solutions to problems you've been working on? Those sudden streams of memory for which you've been searching?

Note them here.

_____

_____

_____

_____

_____

_____

Among the most common responses are:

● alone in nature

● while jogging or long-distance running

● in bed

● lying on a beach

● in the bath or shower

● while on long-haul flights or travelling.

Figure 6.4 Mind Map for when we daydream

The reason these creative outpourings occur in such scenarios (see Figure 6.4) is that our brains are relaxed and either physically or conceptually in solitude. These environments encourage the flowering of creative ideas. So, daydreaming, which was once seen as a no-no, as negative behaviour especially in the classroom – in other words, academically undesirable – we now see as a behaviour that is a fundamentally a magnificently creative exercise. Your average daydream would get you an Oscar if you could convert it into reality!

Daydream believers

If daydreaming is desirable, which it is, what is the difference between the ordinary daydream and the daydream of the very successful or realised brain or genius? Think about it. The difference is that the genius brain daydreams all day just like you do, enjoys daydreaming just like you do, but has one *major* significant advantage: the genius *works to make the dream come true*; the genius works to make that dream a reality. You must do the same.

All the creative geniuses, without exception, in every field, did exactly the same thing: they daydreamed and then worked to make it come true. Thomas Edison's daydream, for instance, was to light

Harness your brain power

the planet Earth at night for all eternity. After 6000 experiments, he achieved his daydream.

Creating a creative brain

Everyone has a creative brain – I do, you do. The trick is to tap into it. How do you do that, though?

We have already noted that creativity flourishes best when you can harmonise the right and left sides of your brain (see page 16). Creative individuals do a number of things that distinguish their thinking from normal untrained or *detrained* thinking.

The key elements of creativity include:

- imagination
- association
- the ability to think at speed
- the ability to be original
- flexibility
- the ability to produce volume.

These elements can be developed easily, like the muscles in your body.

Imagination

Imagination is the engine room of your brain, and in creative individuals their imagination is highly developed.

One of the main ways in which you can develop your imagination is to daydream actively. Also, guide your daydreams so that you are creating the stories in much the same way that Charles Dickens, for example, did when he was writing. Then make those daydreams come true.

Association

Another major element of creative thinking is association. This encompasses the ability to make connections between things.

Because of the linear training many of us receive (see note taking page 104), we tend to think on tramlines, on predetermined tracks, where all the associations are preordained or inevitable or gramatically bound and semantically ruled. That is not the way a creative brain works. A creative brain finds connections between things and then builds on those new connections.

An excellent exercise to encourage this finding of connections between things is, for example, to think of the similarities between a frog and a spaceship (see Figure 6.5).

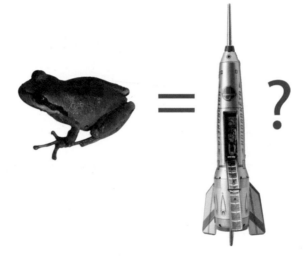

*Figure 6.5 **How many similarities are there between a frog and a spaceship?***

Source: Images taken from POD/Photodisc

Most people will say that there aren't *any* connections between a frog and a spaceship. Spend a minute, though, just thinking of any similarities there might possibly be.

_____

_____

_____

_____

_____

Harness your brain power

Did you come up with any of the following?

- A frog and a spaceship both live in two environments.
- A frog and a spaceship both have launching pads.
- A frog and a spaceship both have a brain (control room).
- A frog and a spaceship both make noise.
- A frog and a spaceship both have television programmes based on them.
- A frog and a spaceship both inspire certain kinds of awe and wonder.
- A frog and a spaceship are both studied by scientists.
- A frog and a spaceship both have sense preceptors.
- A frog and a spaceship both go up and down.
- A frog and a spaceship have both been on the cover of *National Geographic!*

The ability to make connections, to make associations, is a key element of creative thinking.

The ability to think at speed

This is another element of creativity. Creative thinkers think fast. The creative brain thinks fast – even while daydreaming, a lot of the thinking will be fast.

Exercises to try that encourage this include simply thinking of as many uses as you can for any object in one minute. Give yourself this exercise every day, or once or twice a week. Try to think of more per minute each time. Doing this, together with daydreaming, will add arrows to your creative quiver.

The ability to be original

Yet another signpost to the creative brain. To think of ideas that have never been thought of before or been thought of by very very few individuals in slightly different ways is evidence of creativity.

A good creative brain will think of fresh ideas, relish searching for them and inevitably find them. That is because the number of ideas generated so far by human brains, while in the multiple billions, is nowhere near – a fraction of 1 per cent – the number of ideas waiting to be discovered by the next generation of creative brains.

Flexibility

Flexibility is the next major element of creativity. It is the ability to see things from different perspectives.

A 'normal' brain will see things in its default way and always see things in that set way. An example would be watching a football game from a fan's point of view. A creative individual, however, can see that game from a non-fan's viewpoint as well, and would probably write a play or poetry or jokes about it, and 'see' it from very different perspectives. A creative individual will also see the game from the point of view of the ball, or the boot or the goal in relation to the ball, or as a seagull flying over the game. In other words, a creative brain trains itself to see everything from multiple perspectives.

The ability to produce volume

This is the next main factor in creativity – thinking fast and producing quickly. Pablo Picasso, Mozart, and Shakespeare – to name but three – produced masterpieces that poured off the production line of their brains.

Putting them into practice

Each one of the key elements of creativity mentioned above is completely trainable and ties in very comfortably with using the cognitive skills of the cortex (see page 16), as well as with using the multiple intelligences (see page 31).

Creative individuals will always dip into and draw from the multiple intelligences and cognitive skills. If, for example, when using the cognitive skills, you only use words, you will be a very monotonous, boring speaker. If you use those words with rhythm, however, you will be a far more creative speaker. Then, if you use the words with rhythm and images and colour, you will become a great speaker.

In Part 3, I show how key words and key images can become the building blocks of your creativity, remembering and problem solving. Also, how that leads on to the associative explosions of Radiant Thinking® and its ultimate manifestation in Mind Maps. Add the information-sourcing skill of speed reading, together with my unique BOST data-gathering study skills, and you have the fully integrated brain-friendly system needed to enable you to *use your head!*

Mind Mapping is more than a methodology; it is a **philosophy of life**. It will lead you towards **excellence** in whatever you choose to do.

ALEJANDRO CRISTERNA
PRESIDENT, TECMILENIO UNIVERSITY,
MEXICO

Part 3
The essential 'mind tools' for great brains

How good are you at remembering facts? Are you worried about recalling information? Do you want to think and express yourself more creatively?

This part of the book shows you how to use key image words, break out of the straitjacket of linear learning and embrace Radiant Thinking, use the 'Swiss Army knife for the brain' – the Mind Map, speed read and maximise your study skills. These are all 'mind tools' and I will now show you how to use them.

My innovative techniques mimic your brain's innate ways of thinking and will help you to store and retrieve information using the power of imagination and association. As a result, you will have at your disposal a dynamic and organic revision tool, a self-manager in time and a multidimensional mnemonic. You will then be using your head to its full mental potential.

The essential 'mind tools' for great brains

Why key words
are so important

Understanding the power of key words is fundamental for developing creative thinking and problem solving and, as you shall discover in the next chapter, forms the basis of the Mind Map. Here is an exercise to test this and explain why.

EXERCISE 9

Key words

Imagine that your hobby is reading short stories. You read at least five a day and keep notes so that you will not forget any of them. Imagine also that, in order to ensure a proper recall of each story, you use a card filing system. For each story, you have one card for the title and author, then a card for every paragraph. On each of these paragraph cards, you enter a main and a secondary key word or phrase. The key words/phrases you take either directly from the story or make up yourself because they summarise it particularly well.

Imagine, further, that your ten-thousandth story is *Kusa-Hibari* by Lafcadio Hearne and you have prepared the title and author card.

Now read the story below and, for the purpose of this exercise, enter a key recall word or phrase for both the main and secondary idea in the first five paragraphs only (they are numbered), in the space provided on page 97.

Kusa-Hibari by Lafcadio Hearne

(1) His cage is exactly two Japanese inches high and one inch and a half wide: its tiny wooden door, turning upon a pivot, will scarcely admit the tip of my little finger. But he has plenty of room in that cage – room to walk, and jump, and fly, for he is so small that you must look very carefully through the brown-gauze sides of it in order to catch a glimpse of him. I have always to turn the cage round and round, several times, in a good light, before I can discover his whereabouts, and then I usually find him resting in one of the upper corners – clinging, upside down, to his ceiling of gauze.

(2) Imagine a cricket about the size of an ordinary mosquito – with a pair of antennae much longer than his own body, and so fine that you can distinguish them only against the light. Kusa-hibari, or 'grass-lark', is the Japanese name of him; and he is worth in the market exactly twelve cents: that is to say, very much more than his weight in gold. Twelve cents for such a gnat-like thing! ...

(3) By day he sleeps or meditates, except while occupied with the slice of fresh eggplant [aubergine] or cucumber which must be poked into his cage every morning ... to keep him clean and well fed is some-what troublesome: could you see him, you would think it absurd to take any pains for the sake of a creature so ridiculously small.

(4) But always at sunset the infinitesimal soul of him awakens: then the room begins to fill with a delicate and ghostly music of indescribable sweetness – a thin, silvery rippling and trilling as of tiniest electric bells. As the darkness deepens, the sound becomes sweeter – sometimes swelling till the whole house seems to vibrate with the elfish resonance – sometimes thinning down into the faintest imaginable thread of a voice. But loud or low, it keeps a penetrating quality that is weird ... All night the atom thus sings: he ceases only when the temple bell proclaims the hour of dawn.

(5) Now this tiny song is a song of love – vague love of the unseen and unknown. It is quite impossible that he should ever have seen or known, in this present existence of his. Not even his ancestors, for many generations back, could have known anything of the night-life of the fields, or the amorous value of song. They were born of eggs

The essential 'mind tools' for great brains

hatched in a jar of clay, in the shop of some insect-merchant: and they dwelt thereafter only in cages. But he sings the song of his race as it was sung a myriad years ago, and as faultlessly as if he understood the exact significance of every note. Of course he did not learn the song. It is a song of organic memory – deep, dim memory of other quintillions of lives, when the ghost of him shrilled at night from the dewy grasses of the hills. Then that song brought him love and death. He has forgotten all about death: but he remembers the love. And therefore he sings now for the bride that will never come.

(6) So that his longing is unconsciously retrospective: he cries to the dust of the past – he calls to the silence and the gods for the return of time ... Human lovers do very much the same thing without knowing it. They call their illusion an Ideal: and their Ideal is, after all, a mere shadowing of race-experience, a phantom of organic memory. The living present has very little to do with it ... Perhaps his atom also has an ideal, or at least the rudiment of an ideal; but, in any event, the tiny desire must utter its plaint in vain.

(7) The fault is not altogether mine. I had been warned that if the creature were mated, he would cease to sing and would speedily die. But, night after night, the plaintive, sweet, unanswered trilling touched me like a reproach – became at last an obsession, an affliction, a torment of conscience; and I tried to buy a female. It was too late in the season; there were no more kusa-hibari for sale, either males or females. The insect-merchant laughed and said, 'He ought to have died about the twentieth day of the ninth month.' (It was already the second day of the tenth month.) But the insect merchant did not know that I have a good stove in my study, and keep the temperature at above 75°F. Wherefore my grass-lark still sings at the close of the eleventh month, and I hope to keep him alive until the Period of Greatest Cold. However, the rest of his generation are probably dead: neither for love nor money could I now find him a mate. And were I to set him free in order that he might make the search for himself, he could not possibly live through a single night, even if fortunate enough to escape by day the multitude of his natural enemies in the garden – ants, centipedes, and ghastly earth-spiders.

(8) Last evening – the twenty-ninth of the eleventh month – an odd feeling came to me as I sat at my desk: a sense of emptiness in the room. Then I became aware that my grass-lark was silent, contrary to his wont. I went to the silent cage, and found him lying dead beside a dried-up lump of eggplant as grey and hard as a stone. Evidently he had not been fed for three or four days; but only the night before his death he had been singing wonderfully so that I foolishly imagined him to be more than usually contented. My student, Aki, who loves insects, used to feed him; but Aki had gone into the country for a week's holiday, and the duty of caring for the grass-lark had devolved upon Hana, the housemaid. She is not sympathetic, Hana the housemaid. She says that she did not forget the mite – but there was no more eggplant. And she had never thought of substituting a slice of onion or of cucumber! ...
I spoke words of reproof to Hana the housemaid and she dutifully expressed contrition. But the fairy-music had stopped: and the stillness reproaches; and the room is cold, in spite of the stove.

(9) Absurd! ... I have made a good girl unhappy because of an insect half the size of a barley grain! The quenching of that infinitesimal life troubled me more than I could have believed possible ... Of course, the mere habit of thinking about a creature's wants – even the wants of a cricket – may create, by insensible degrees, an imaginative interest, an attachment of which one becomes conscious only when the relation is broken. Besides, I had felt so much, in the hush of the night, the charm of the delicate voice – telling of one minute existence dependent upon my will and selfish pleasure, as upon the favour of a god – telling me also that the atom of ghost in the tiny cage, and the atom of ghost within myself, were forever but one and the same in the deeps of the Vast of being ... And then to think of the little creature hungering and thirsting, night after night and day after day, while the thoughts of his guardian deity were turned to the weaving of dreams! ... How bravely, nevertheless, he sang on to the very end – an atrocious end, for he had eaten his own legs! ... May the gods forgive us all – especially Hana the housemaid!

(10) Yet, after all, to devour one's own legs for hunger is not the worst that can happen to a being cursed with the gift of song. There are human crickets who must eat their own hearts in order to sing.

The essential 'mind tools' for great brains

Key words or phrases for main and secondary ideas from Kusa-Hibari

Paragraph	Main	Secondary
1		
2		
3		
4		
5		

In the next table you will find sample key words and phrases from the notes made by students who have previously done this exercise. Briefly compare and contrast them with your own ideas.

Students' suggested key words and phrases

Paragraph	Main	Secondary
1	his cage wooden door ceiling of gauze small insect	two Japanese inches turning plenty of room discover whereabouts
2	cricket weight in gold antennae kusa-hibari	grass-lark twelve cents market gnat-like
3	sleep clean and well fed occupied absurd	fresh cucumber pains meditation small

▶

4	penetrating	silvery rippling
	music	house vibrating
	electric bells	penetrating
	soul	hour of dawn
5	love	night-life
	amorous	insect merchant
	the hills	significance
	death	love and death

In class situations, instructors then circled one word from each section. Their choices are shown in the next table.

Instructors' choices of students' key words and phrases

Paragraph	Main	Secondary
1	wooden door	discover whereabouts
2	weight in gold	market
3	occupied	pains
4	penetrating	hour of dawn
5	love	night-life

The students were then asked to explain why, in the context of the exercise, those words and phrases and not others had been selected by the instructors. Their answers usually included the following reasons: 'good image words', 'imaginative', 'descriptive', 'appropriate', 'good for remembering', 'evocative' and so on.

Only one student in 50 realised why the instructors had really chosen those words: and in the context of the exercise the series chosen was disastrous.

To understand why, it is necessary to imagine a time some years after the story has been read, when you go to look at the notes again for recall purposes. Imagine that some friends have played a prank, taking out the title cards of some of your stories and challenging you to remember the titles and authors. You would have no idea to start with which story your cards referred to and would have to rely solely on them to give you back the correct images.

With the key words the instructors chose, you would probably be forced to link them in the following way: 'wooden door', a general phrase, would gain a mystery story air when you read 'discover whereabouts'. The next two key words – 'weight in gold' and 'market' – would confirm this, adding a further touch of intrigue, suggesting a criminal activity. The next three key words – 'occupied', 'pains' and 'penetrating' – might lead you to assume that one of the characters, perhaps the hero, was personally in difficulty, adding further tension to the ongoing plot as the 'hour of dawn', obviously an important and suspense-filled moment in the story, approached. The next key words – 'love' and 'night-life' – would add a romantic or risqué touch to the whole affair, encouraging you to thumb quickly through the remaining key words in search of further adventures and climaxes! You would have created an interesting new story, but would not remember the original one.

Words that seemed quite good at the time have not, for some reason, proved adequate for recall. To explain why, it is necessary to discuss the difference between key recall words and key creative words and the way in which they interact after a period of time has passed.

Good recall words would have been the ones shown in the next table.

Good recall words

Paragraph	Main	Secondary
1	cage	two Japanese inches
2	cricket	grass-lark
3	sleep	fresh cucumber
4	music	house vibrating
5	song	amorous value

Understanding why these words are better for recall involves thinking about the way in which the human brain processes information. The Mind Map shown in Figure 7.1 magnificently summarises the content but also the feelings and emotions of the *Kusa-Hibari* story. It is a superb example of the way in which colour, code, form and image can be used to encapsulate an entire story (see Chapter 8 for more on Mind Maps).

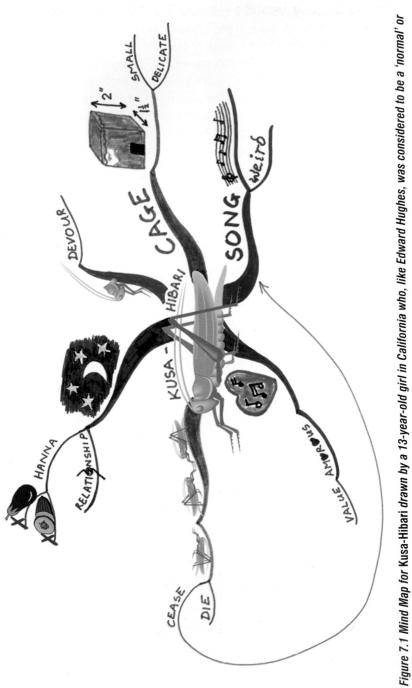

Figure 7.1 Mind Map for Kusa-Hibari drawn by a 13-year-old girl in California who, like Edward Hughes, was considered to be a 'normal' or 'average' student

Types of key words – recall and creative

A key *recall* word or phrase is one that funnels into itself a wide range of special images and, when it is triggered, funnels back the *same* images. It will tend to be a strong noun or verb, on occasion surrounded by additional key adjectives or adverbs (see Figure 7.2).

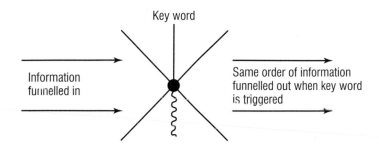

Key word

Information funnelled in

Same order of information funnelled out when key word is triggered

Figure 7.2 Diagram representing a key recall word

A *creative* word is one that is particularly evocative and forms images. It is also far more general than the more directed key recall word. Words like 'ooze' and 'bizarre' are especially evocative but do not necessarily bring to mind a specific image (see Figure 7.3).

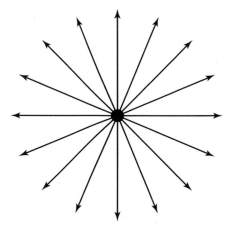

Figure 7.3 A key creative word sprays out associations in all directions

Apart from understanding the difference between recall and creative words, it is also necessary to understand the nature of words themselves and the nature of your brain, which uses them (see also pages 115–16 for more analysis of key words and key images in relation to Mind Maps).

The multiordinate nature of words

Every word is 'multiordinate', which simply means that each word is like a little centre from which emanate many, many little hooks (see Figure 7.4). Each hook can attach to other words to give both words in the new pair slightly different meanings. For example the word 'run' can be hooked quite differently to form 'run like hell' and 'her stocking has a run in it'.

In addition to the multiordinate nature of words, our brains are all different from each other. As shown in Chapter 1, the number of connections your brain can make within itself is almost *infinite*. Each individual also experiences a very different life from that of other individuals (even if two people are enjoying the 'same experience' together, they are in very different worlds – that is, *A* is enjoying the experience with *B* as a major part of it and *B* is enjoying the experience with *A* as a major part of it).

Similarly, the associations that each person will have for any word will be different from everybody else's. Even a simple word such as 'leaf' will produce a different series of images for each person who reads or hears it. A person whose favourite colour is green, for example, might imagine the general greenness of leaves; someone whose favourite colour is brown, the beauty of autumn; a person who had been injured falling out of a tree, the feeling of fear; a gardener, the different emotions connected with the pleasure of seeing leaves grow and the thought of humus and building a compost heap when they have fallen, and so on. I could go on for ever and still not satisfy the range of associations that you, reading this book, might have when you think of leaves.

As well as the unique way in which your mind sees its personal images, each brain is also, by nature, both creative and self-organising. It will tend to 'tell itself interesting and entertaining stories', as it does, for example, when we daydream or dream at night.

Figure 7.4 *Each word is multiordinate – that is, it has a large number of hooks (top). Because of this characteristic, your mind can easily follow the wrong series of connections, especially with creative words (centre). When proper key recall words are used, however, your mind will make the right connections (bottom)*

The reason the recall and general words selected from *Kusa-Hibari* were not effective can now clearly be seen. When each of the multiordinate words or phrases is approached, your mind automatically picked the connecting hooks that were most obvious, produced most images or made the most sense.

Consequently, your mind was led down a path that was more creative than recall-based and a story was constructed that was interesting, but hardly useful for remembering.

Key recall words force your mind to make the proper links in the right direction, enabling it to recreate the story even if, to all other intents and purposes, it has been forgotten.

Key concept overview: restructuring note taking

The main body your recalling is of this key concept nature. It is not, as is often assumed, a word-for-word verbatim process.

When people describe books they have read or places they have been to, they do not start to 'reread' from memory. Instead, they give key concept overviews, outlining the main characters, settings and events, then add descriptive details. Similarly, the single key word or phrase will bring back whole ranges of experience and sensation. Think, for example, of the range of images that enter your mind when you read the word 'child'.

How, then, does acceptance of these facts about key recall words affect our attitude towards the structure of note taking?

Because we have all become so used to speaking and writing words, we mistakenly assume that the normal sentence structure is the best way to remember verbal images and ideas. Thus, the majority of students and even graduates take notes in a normal literary fashion similar to the example of a university student's notes (mine!) shown in Figure 7.5, which were rated 'good' by the professor.

At the time, I thought that I was good at note taking, but, if you look at these notes, you realise that the information is very difficult to extract from them. They may look 'neat' in a traditional note taking sense, but they are very messy in terms of your brain being able to extract the information from them. The notes are the opposite of brain-friendly - they are brain-*un*friendly.

Indeed, it was the fact that I was making these kinds of notes at the time and getting worse and worse in terms of my academic performance which was one of the main triggers to my developing of Mind Maps.

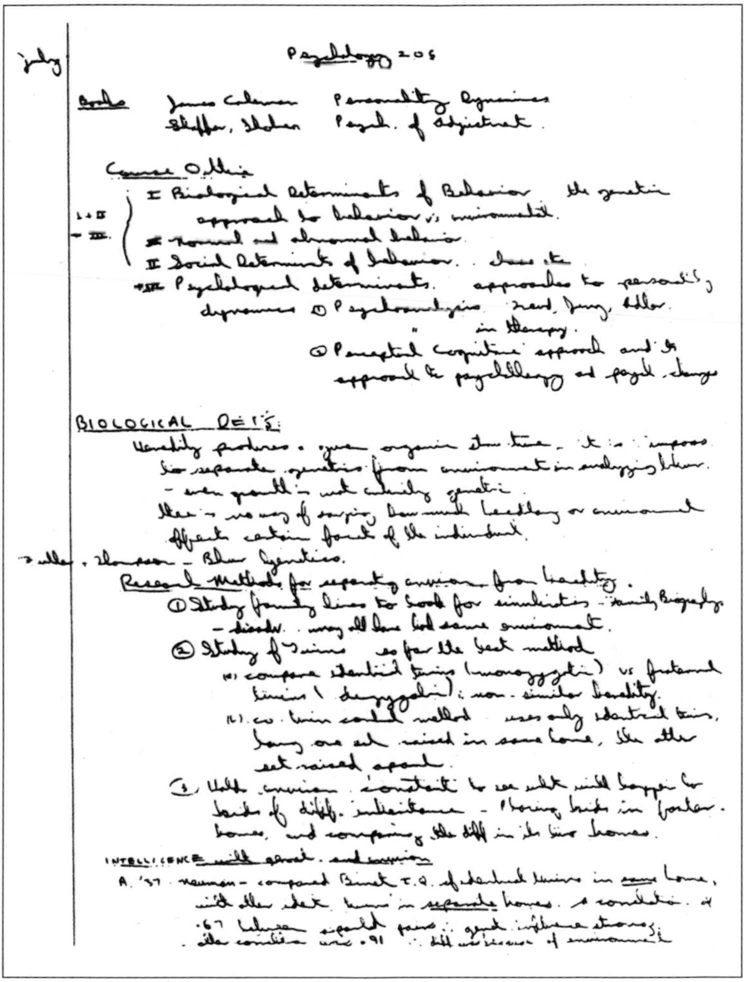

Figure 7.5 An example of a student's traditionally 'good' university notes (in this case, these are my own notes!)

Our new knowledge of key concepts and recall shows that, which these types of notes, 90 per cent of the words are not necessary for recall purposes. This frighteningly high figure becomes even more frightening when we take a closer look at what happens with standard sentence-type notes.

- Time is wasted recording words that have no bearing on memory (estimated waste – 90 per cent).

- Time is wasted rereading the same unnecessary words (estimated waste – 90 per cent).

- Time is wasted searching for the words that are key recall words, for they are usually not distinguished by any marks and so blend in with the other non-recall words.

- The connections between key recall words are interrupted by words that separate them. We know that memory works by association and any interference from non-recall words makes the connections less strong.

- The key recall words are separated in time by intervening words – after one key word or phrase has been read, it takes at least a few seconds to get to the next one. The longer the time between connections, the less chance there is that proper connections will be made.

- The key recall words are separated in space, too, by their distance from each other on the page. As in the previous point, the greater the distance between the words, the less chance there is of a proper connection being made.

You are therefore advised to practise selecting key recall words and phrases from any previous notes you have made during periods of study. It will also be helpful at this point for you to summarise this chapter in key note form (see also page 135).

In addition, reconsider your key recall and creative words in the light of the information given in Chapter 5 on memory, especially the section dealing with mnemonic principles. That chapter can itself be reconsidered in the light of this chapter, putting an emphasis on the relationship and similarities between mnemonic systems and key and creative concepts.

The review graph (see Figure 4.8) is another important consideration. Review is made much easier when notes are in key form, because less time is expended and your recall will be superior and more complete. Any weak linkages will also be made stronger and cemented in the early stages.

Finally, linkages between key recall words and concepts should always be emphasised and, where possible, simple lists and lines of key words should be avoided.

What has been explained here about key recall word linking and patterning is the precursor to the Mind Mapping technique. In the next chapter, we shall further explore key words and key images and their linking and patterning. We shall look at Radiant Thinking, too, and how everything comes together in the ultimate thinking tool for your brain – the Mind Map.

The Mind Map is a manifestation of both *imagination* and *association*, combining the main principles you have been learning about in this chapter and Chapter 5. A Mind Map is a multidimensional mnemonic, as well as being an infinitely explosive creative thinking technique.

Introducing Mind Maps and Radiant Thinking

This chapter delves deeper into the non-linear nature of your brain, and then goes on to explain how Mind Maps stimulate whole-brain and Radiant Thinking. Following from this, the theory and method for making Mind Maps are fully outlined. Mind Maps enabled me to write *Use Your Head!*

What is a Mind Map?

A Mind Map is a graphically and visually interlaced thinking tool for storing, organising, prioritising and outputting information. As mentioned earlier, it has been called the 'Swiss Army knife for the brain'.

The process of Mind Mapping mimics the way your brain connects and processes information. You can create a Mind Map on paper or onscreen (with software such as iMindMap – see Appendix for more details) using key or trigger words and images, each of which will 'snap on' specific memories and encourage new thoughts and ideas. Each of the memory triggers in a Mind Map is a key to unlocking facts, ideas and information. These triggers also enable you to release the true potential of your amazing mind.

The clue to the Mind Map's effectiveness lies in its dynamic shape and form. It mimics a brain cell under the microscope and is designed to encourage your brain to work in a way that is fast, efficient and in the style that it does naturally.

Every time we look at the veins of a leaf or the branches of a tree, we see *nature's* Mind Maps, echoing the shapes of brain cells and reflecting the way we ourselves are created and connected. Like us, the natural world is forever changing and regenerating and has a communication structure that appears similar to our own. Thus, a Mind Map is a natural thinking tool that draws on the inspiration and effectiveness of these natural structures.

Mind Maps are particularly adaptive for reading, revising, note taking, note making and planning efficiently. They are invaluable for gathering and ordering information and identifying the key trigger words and facts from:

- reference books, textbooks, papers, journals, the Internet

- seminars, conferences, presentations, meetings

- your own head.

They help you to manage information effectively and increase the potential for success.

Before I show you how to prepare and create a Mind Map, there are some important facts you need to know about how your brain thinks that link directly to the structure of Mind Maps. First of all, try this exercise.

EXERCISE 10

Space travel

Prepare a half-hour speech on the topic of space travel on a piece of paper, starting immediately after you have read these instructions.

Allow no more than five minutes for the task, whether or not you have finished. Make a note of any problems you have with organising your thoughts when performing this task. This exercise is referred to later in this chapter.

The essential 'mind tools' for great brains

The linear straitjacket

For the last few hundred years, it has been popularly thought that our minds work in a linear or list-like manner. This belief arose primarily because of the increasing reliance on our two main methods of communication – namely, speech and print.

In speech, we are restricted, by the nature of time and space, to speaking and hearing one word at a time. Speech has often thus been seen as a linear or line-like process between people (see Figure 8.1).

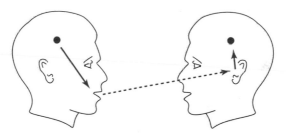

*Figure 8.1 **Speech has traditionally been seen as a list-like affair***

Print has generally been viewed as even more linear. Not only is the individual forced to take in units of print in consecutive order, but print was traditionally laid out in a series of lines or rows of type per page.

This linear emphasis overflowed into normal writing or note making. Virtually everyone was (and still is) trained in school to take notes in sentences or vertical lists (see Figures 8.2a and b). Indeed, you, like most other readers, will probably have prepared your half-hour speech on space travel in one of these two ways.

The acceptance of this way of thinking is so long-standing that little has been done to contradict it. Think about it, though – what in the natural world is absolutely straight? The same is true for human physiology and intelligence. We don't naturally think in straight lines, so why on earth do we scan or write in straight, horizontal, diagonal and vertical lines?

Recent evidence shows your brain to be far more multidimensional and fond of making patterns than this, suggesting that there must be fundamental flaws in the speech and print views.

Figure 8.2 Standard forms of 'good' or 'neat' notes:
(a) Normal line structure – sentence-based
(b) Standard list structure – order-of-importance-based

The essential 'mind tools' for great brains

The argument that the brain functions linearly because of the speech patterns it has evolved fails to consider, as do the supporters of the absolute nature of IQ tests, the nature of the organism itself. It is easy to point out that when words travel from one person to another, they necessarily do so in a line, but that is not really the point. More relevant is the question, 'How does the brain of the person speaking and the brain of the person receiving the words deal with them *internally?*'

The answer is that your brain is most certainly *not* dealing with them in simple lists and lines. You can verify this by thinking of the way in which your own thought processes work while you are speaking to someone else. You will observe that, although a single line of words is coming out, a continuing and enormously complex process of sorting and selecting is taking place in your mind throughout the conversation. Whole networks of words and ideas are being juggled and interlinked in order to communicate a certain meaning to your listener.

Similarly, your listener is not simply observing a long list of words like someone sucking up spaghetti. He or she is receiving each word in the context of the words that surround it. At the same time your listener is also giving the multiordinate nature of each word his or her own special interpretation as dictated by the structure of that person's unique information patterns and will be analysing, coding and criticising throughout the process (see Figure 8.3).

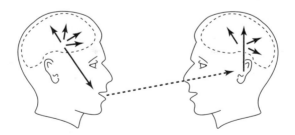

Figure 8.3 It is the network inside the mind, not the simple order in which words are presented, that is more important to an understanding of how we relate to words

You may have noticed people suddenly reacting negatively to words that you liked or thought were harmless. They react that way because the associations *they* have for those words are different from yours. Knowing that will help you understand more clearly the nature of conversations, disagreements and misunderstandings.

The argument for print is also weak. Despite the fact that we are trained to read units of information one after another, that these are presented in lines and that we therefore write and make notes in lines, linear presentation is not necessary for understanding and, in many instances, is a disadvantage.

Your mind is perfectly capable of taking in information that is non-linear. In its day-to-day life, it does so nearly all the time, observing all those things that surround it, which include common, non-linear forms of print – photographs, illustrations, diagrams and so on. It is only our society's enormous reliance on linear information that has muddied the issue. The limitation of linear thinking is that it can take quite a while to get to the core issue of the matter and, during the process, you will say, hear or read a great deal that is not essential for long-term recall.

Linear v. whole-brain thinking

Your brain's non-linear character is further confirmed by recent bio-chemical, physiological and psychological research. Each of these areas of research is discovering, to its amazement and restrained delight, that your brain is non-linear and so complex and interlinked, it guarantees centuries of exhilarating research and exploration.

Your brain is multidimensional and perfectly capable of – indeed, *designed for* – taking in information that is non-linear. It does so all the time – when looking at photographs, pictures or interpreting the images and environment that are around you every day. Your brain, when listening to a series of spoken sentences, does not absorb information word by word, line by line; it takes in the information as a whole, sorts it, interprets it and feeds it back to you in a multitude of ways.

So, your brain handles information better if the information is designed to 'slot in' – remember the left and right cortex research of Roger Sperry, Robert Ornstein and Eran Zaidel (see page 16). That research alone leads anyone who thinks about it to conclude that a note making and thought organisation technique designed to satisfy the needs of the whole brain would have to include words, numbers,

The essential 'mind tools' for great brains

sequence and linearity, as well as colour, dimension, visual rhythms, spatial awareness and so on – in other words, Mind Maps!

From whatever perspective you approach the question – be it from the nature of words and information, the function of recall during learning, holographic models of the brain or recent brain research – the conclusions in the end are identical: in order to utilise fully the capacity of our brain, we need to consider each of the elements that add up to the whole and integrate them in a unified way. In other words, combine the left-side with the right-side functions across the corpus callosum to create whole-brain thinking. (Whole-brain thinking is also exactly the premise of my BOST programme – see Chapter 12.)

Key words and key images

The word 'key' in front of the words 'word' or 'image' means much more than 'this is important'. It means, this is a 'memory key'. The key word or key image is being developed as a critically important trigger to stimulate your mind and unlock and retrieve your memories. You hear each word and put it in the context of existing knowledge, as well as the other words around it. You do not need to have heard the entire range of sentences before forming a response. Key words are therefore critical 'signposts' or 'joggers' to your multidimensional data sorter – your brain (see also Chapter 7).

A key word is a special word that has been chosen or created to become a unique reference point for something important that you wish to remember. Words stimulate the left side of your brain and are a vital component in mastering memory, but they are not as powerful on their own as when you take the time to draw them and transform them into a key image. An effective key image will stimulate *both* sides of your brain and draw on all your senses. Key images are at the very heart of Mind Maps and the BOST programme.

Here is a simple example of how a key word and key image can boost your memory.

● When trying to find an image to encapsulate the concept of environmental water and waste management and the problems of water shortage, you might choose the word 'tap'.

- The word 'tap' will, as a key word, trigger your analytical left-brain memory.

- Drawing a picture of a tap with, perhaps, a drop of water dripping out, will create a key image, which will engage your visual right-brain memory.

- The picture will become a visual trigger that will represent the written word, plus water and waste management as an industry, with its attendant hosepipe bans, leaking pipes and declining reservoir reserves.

The word 'tap' on its own is not enough to trigger the recall of *all* your studies of water energy, because it does not engage your whole brain. The word as part of a sentence will not trigger the entire experience either, because a sentence defines and limits. Rather, the purpose of a key word that has been transformed into a drawn key image is to connect with both your left-brain and the right-brain functions. That action radiates connections and triggers your recall of complete associated information.

Key words and their context are vitally important memory joggers and it is the network inside your mind that is of most importance in helping to understand and interpret them.

To help you understand how key words are so effective in the framework of a Mind Map, you need to be introduced to the principles of Radiant Thinking and Basic Ordering Ideas.

What is Radiant Thinking?

To understand why Mind Maps are so effective, it is helpful to know more about the way your brain thinks and remembers information. As explained above, your brain does not think in a linear, monotonous way, but, rather, in multiple directions simultaneously – starting from the central trigger points found in key images and key words. That process is Radiant Thinking.

As the term suggests, thoughts radiate outwards like the branches of a tree, the veins of a leaf or the blood vessels of the body emanating from the heart. In the same way, a Mind Map starts with the central concept and radiates outwards to take in the detail, mirroring effectively the activity of your brain.

The more closely you can record information in a way that reflects the natural workings of your brain, the more efficiently your brain will be able to trigger the recall of essential facts and personal memories. To show you what I mean, try the following exercise.

EXERCISE 11

Radiant Thinking

Most people believe that the brain thinks linguistically. I am going to ask you to access a piece of data from that vast database of yours – your brain. You will have no time to think about it in advance. I would like you to consider the following questions, once you have accessed the piece of data below.

- What was it that you accessed?
- How long did it take you to access it?
- Was there colour?
- What were the associations around the data?

Now, here is the data: banana.

When you 'heard' the word you may have seen the colours yellow, brown or green, depending on the ripeness of the fruit. You may have seen its curved shape. You may have associated the image with a fruit salad, breakfast cereal or a milkshake. The image will have appeared instantaneously, as if from nowhere, and you are unlikely to have spent any time visualising the letters of the word. The image was already stored in your mind; you simply needed to trigger its release.

What you have learned from the exercise is that, primarily, fundamentally, we think in images. Words are a subroutine that carry essential images between our brains. Also, that everyone, whatever their sex, status or nationality, uses Radiant Thinking to link key word associations with key images – instantaneously. That process is the basis of all our thinking and the basis of Mind Maps. Indeed, Mind Maps have been devised to enhance and increase your Radiant Thinking processes.

Basic Ordering Ideas (BOIs)

You now need to add structure to the Mind Maps of your ideas.

The first step in building a Mind Map is to decide on your Basic Ordering Ideas (BOIs). BOIs are the 'hooks' on which to hang all associated ideas, just as the chapter headings of a textbook represent the thematic content within its pages. BOIs are the chapter headings of your thoughts – the words or images that represent the simplest and most obvious categories of information. They are the words that will automatically cause your brain to think of the greatest number of associations.

If you are not sure what your BOIs should be, ask yourself the following simple questions with regard to your main goal or vision.

- What knowledge is required to achieve my aim?

- If this were a book, what would the chapter headings be?

- What are my specific objectives?

- What are the seven most important categories in that subject area?

- What are the answers to my seven basic questions: why, what, where, who, how, which, when?

- Is there a larger, more encompassing, category all of these fit into that it would be more appropriate to use?

For example, a Mind Map of life plans might include the following useful personal BOI categories:

- personal history – past, present, future

- strengths

- weaknesses

- likes

- dislikes

- long-term goals

- family

- friends

- achievements

- hobbies

- emotions

- work

- home

- responsibilities.

The advantages of having well thought out BOIs are that:

- the primary ideas are in place, so the secondary ideas will follow and flow more naturally than would be the case without them

- the BOIs help to shape, sculpt and construct your Mind Maps, so encourage your mind to think in a naturally structured way.

When you decide on your first set of BOIs before you begin your Mind Map, the rest of your ideas will flow in a coherent and useful way. Below, we will show how to use a Mind Map for Exercise 10, about space travel that you did earlier, and how to construct your own for a CV later, to help you test your application of BOIs as well as get used to the idea of consciously thinking pictorially and in colour.

Your brain and Mind Mapping

If your brain is to relate to information as efficiently as possible the information must be structured in such a way that it will 'slot in' as easily as possible. It follows that if your brain works primarily with key concepts in an interlinked and integrated manner, your notes and your word relations should, in many instances, be structured in that way rather than in traditional 'lines'.

Rather than starting from the top and working down in sentences or lists, you should start from the centre with the main idea and branch out as dictated by the individual ideas and general form of the central theme.

Referring back to Exercise 10, which you worked on on page 110, Figure 8.4 gives an example of how it might be tackled using a Mind Map (this one has been created using iMindMap software by World Mind Mapping Champion Phil Chambers).

You can now begin to see a number of advantages of Mind Maps over the linear form of note taking that you tried out at the beginning of the chapter.

- The centre, with the main idea, is clearly defined.

- The relative importance of each idea is clearly indicated. More important ideas will be nearer the centre and less important ideas will be near the edge.

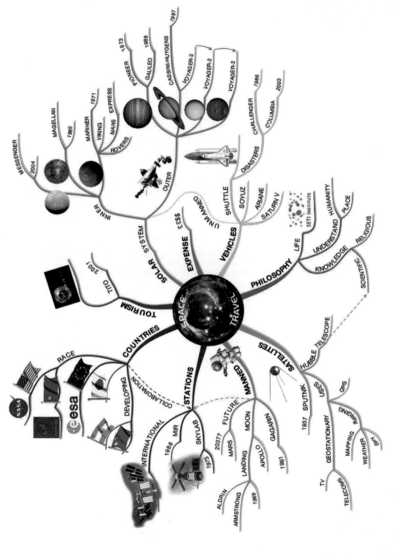

Figure 8.4 Initial ideas Mind Mapped around a central theme (in this case, space travel)

- The links between the key concepts are immediately recognisable because of their proximity and connections.

- As a result of the above, recall and review are both more effective and rapid.

- The nature of the structure allows for new information to be added easily, without messy crossing out, squeezing in and so on.

- Each Mind Map made will look and be different from each other Mind Map. That will aid recall.

- In the more creative areas of note making, the open-ended nature of Mind Maps enables your brain to make new connections readily.

In connection with these points – especially the last one – you should now do an exercise similar to your space travel speech at the beginning of this chapter. This time, create your own Mind Map rather than rely on more linear methods. You could try a simple 'things to do' exercise or, perhaps, a more detailed CV or work experience brainstorm. Examples of these are shown in the next chapter, which further develops the process of how to create a Mind Map step by step.

How to create a Mind Map

In this chapter, I shall show you how to create a hand-drawn Mind Map (for more detailed instructions and how to prepare and create an iMindMap, see *The Mind Map Book* (BBC Active, 2010) and visit **www.thinkbuzan.com** and see 'Products' tab).

Here are the steps that you need to follow.

1 Focus on the core question, the precise topic (things to do or work/life balance, for example). Be clear about what it is that you are aiming for or trying to resolve.

2 Turn your first sheet of paper sideways in front of you, landscape-style, in order to start creating your Mind Map in the centre of the page. This orientation will allow you freedom of expression, without being restricted by the narrow measure of a page the normal way up – portrait.

3 Draw an image in the centre of the blank sheet of paper to represent your goal. Don't worry if you feel that you can't draw well; that doesn't matter. It is very important to use an image as the starting point for your Mind Map because an image will jump-start your thinking by activating your imagination.

4 Use colour from the outset – for emphasis, structure, texture, creativity – to stimulate visual flow and reinforce the image in your mind. Try to use at least three colours overall and

create your own colour-coding system. Colour can be used hierarchically or thematically or it can be used to emphasise certain points.

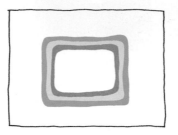

5 Now draw a series of thick, differently coloured lines radiating from the centre of the image. They are the primary branches of your Mind Map and will support your Basic Ordering Ideas like the sturdy branches of a tree. Make sure that you connect those primary branches firmly to your central image because your brain, and therefore your memory, operates by association.

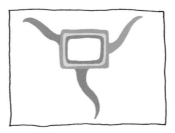

6 Curve your lines because they are more interesting to the eye and more memorable for your brain than straight ones.

7 Write one key word that you associate with the topic on each branch. Each key word represents your main thought (and your Basic Ordering Idea), relating to themes such as situation, feelings, facts and choices. Remember, using only *one* key word per line allows you to define the very essence of the issue you are exploring, while also helping ensure that the association is stored in your brain as emphatically as possible. Phrases and sentences limit the effect and confuse your memory.

The essential 'mind tools' for great brains

8 Add a few empty branches to your Mind Map. That stimulates and provokes your brain to put something on them.

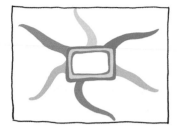

9 Next, create second- and third-level branches for your related associated and secondary thoughts. The secondary level connects to the primary branches, the third level to the secondary branches and so on. Association is everything in this process. The words that you choose for each of your branches might include themes that ask questions – the who, what, where, why, how of the subject or situation.

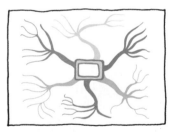

EXERCISE 12

Create your own Mind Map
Now you have the rudimentary skills you can create your own Mind Map. Use the Mind Map laws on page 128 and copy the style (not the substance) used in Figures 9.1 and 9.2 overleaf, showing Mind Maps about the author, to prepare your own Mind Map CV.
    Start the exercise now.

Figure 9.1 A CV Mind Map for me in hand-drawn form.

The essential 'mind tools' for great brains

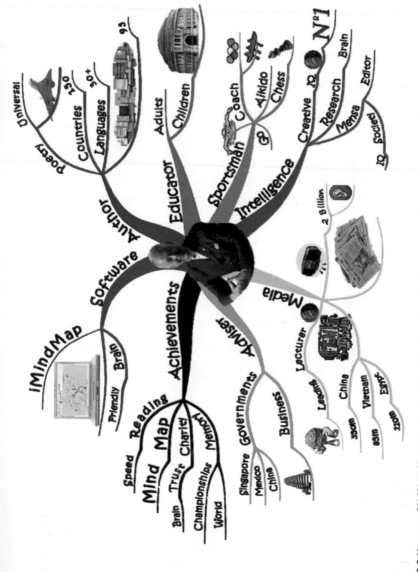

Figure 9.2 Here my CV Mind Map is presented in iMindMap form to show you the tremendous range of possible styles

Mind Maps – the natural laws

- Start with a coloured image in the centre. An image often *is* worth a thousand words and encourages creative thought while significantly increasing memory. Place the paper horizontally so it is in a landscape orientation.

- Include images throughout your Mind Map. This is for the reasons given above and to stimulate all cortical processes, attract your eye and aid memory.

- Words should be printed rather than joined up. This is for reading back purposes, a printed word gives a more photographic, clear, legible image and more comprehensive feedback. The little extra time that it takes to print is amply made up for in the time saved when reading back.

- The printed words should be on branches and each branch connected to other thinner branches. That guarantees the Mind Map has a basic structure.

- Words should be in 'units' – that is, one word per line. It leaves each word with more free hooks and allows note making more freedom and flexibility than including more words would do.

- Use colours throughout your Mind Map as they enhance memory, delight the eye and stimulate the cortical processes.

Mind Maps have a structure that encourages your mind to be as free as possible. The idea is to recall everything your mind thinks of around the central idea. As your mind will generate ideas faster than you can write, there should be almost no pause. Indeed, if you do pause, you will probably notice that your pen or pencil dithers over the page. The moment you notice it happening, get it back down and carry on. Do not worry about order or organisation as they will, in most cases, take care of themselves. If they don't, a final bit of reordering can be completed at the end of the exercise.

Mind Maps can therefore be seen to eliminate all the disadvantages of standard note making outlined on pages 104–7.

The essential 'mind tools' for great brains

Solving problems with Mind Maps

Problems often noted in the space travel exercise, completed in the previous chapter (see page 110) include those with:

- order
- logical sequence
- beginning
- ending

- organisation
- time distribution
- emphasis of ideas
- mental blocks.

Problems in these areas arise because people attempt to select the main headings and ideas one after the other and put them into order as they go. So, they try to order the structure of their speech without having considered all the information available. Doing so will inevitably lead to confusion and the problems noted, for new information that turns up after the first few items have been noted might suddenly alter the person's whole outlook on the subject. With standard note taking and note making, these types of mental events are disruptive. With the Mind Map approach, however, it is simply part of the overall process and can be handled properly and straightforwardly.

Another disadvantage of the list-like method is that it operates against the way in which your brain works. Each time an idea is thought of, it is put on the list and forgotten while a new idea is searched out. That means all the multiordinate and associative possibilities of each word are cut off and boxed away while the mind wanders around in search of another new idea. The Mind Map approach, however, enables each idea to be left as a totally open possibility so that the Mind Map grows organically and can increase rather than be constrained.

Some examples of Mind Maps

You might find it interesting to compare your efforts so far with those of three schoolchildren shown in Figures 9.3, 9.4 and 9.5.

Figure 9.3 shows the normal writing of a 14-year-old boy who was described as reasonably bright, but messy, confused and mentally disorganised. The example of his linear writing represents his 'best notes' and explains clearly why he was described as he was.

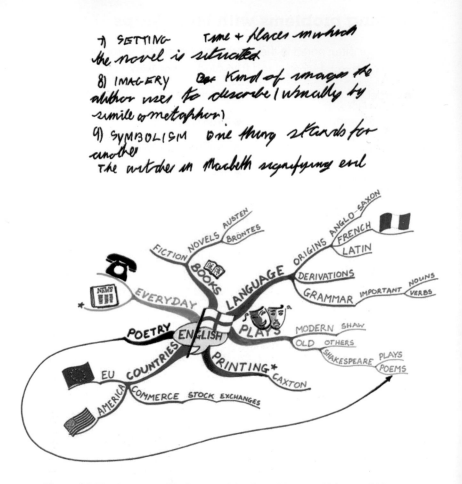

7) SETTING   Time + Places in which
the novel is situated

8) IMAGERY   the Kind of image the
author uses to describe (usually by
simile or metaphor)

9) SYMBOLISM   One thing stands for
another
The witches in Macbeth signifying evil

NOVELS AUSTEN
FICTION BRONTES
BOOKS
EVERYDAY
NEWS

LANGUAGE ORIGINS ANGLO-SAXON
FRENCH
LATIN
DERIVATIONS
GRAMMAR IMPORTANT NOUNS
VERBS

POETRY ENGLISH PLAYS
MODERN SHAW
OLD OTHERS
SHAKESPEARE PLAYS
POEMS

EU COUNTRIES
PRINTING*
CAXTON
AMERICA COMMERCE STOCK EXCHANGES

Figure 9.3 The best notes' in linear writing by a 14-year-old-boy and his Mind Map notes in English

The Mind Map of English that he completed in ten minutes shows almost completely the reverse, suggesting that we can often mis-judge a child simply because of the method we require him or her to use to express ideas.

The example in Figure 9.4 is a Mind Map by a student who twice failed GCSE economics and was described by the teacher as having enormous thinking and learning problems, combined with an almost total lack of knowledge of his subject. The Mind Map, which was completed in five minutes, shows quite the reverse.

The essential 'mind tools' for great brains

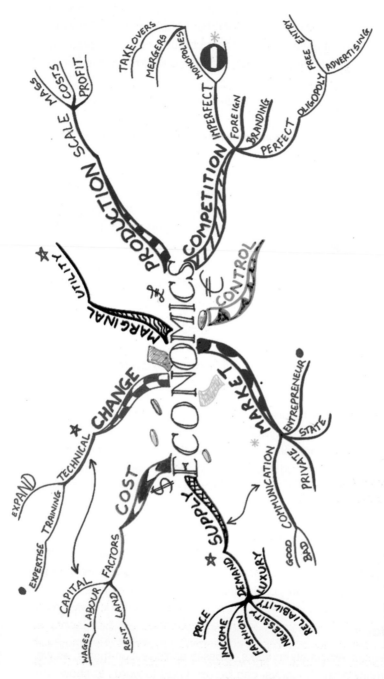

Figure 9.4 Mind Map by a student who twice failed his GCSE economics exams

The Mind Map in Figure 9.5 was completed by an A-level student for pure mathematics. When her Mind Map was shown to a professor of mathematics, he thought that it had been done by a university student and probably took two days to complete. In fact, it took her only 20 minutes.

The Mind Map enabled her to display an extraordinary level of creativity about a subject that is normally considered dry, dull and oppressive. It could have been made even better by ensuring that each line contained only 'units' of words instead of phrases. Her use of form and shape to augment the words indicates the diversity possible in these Mind Map structures.

Finally, Figures 9.6 and 9.7 show two more example of Mind Maps that represent this whole-brain thinking method for making notes. They also summarise parts of the book.

In these Mind Maps, key recall words and images are linked to each other around a main central image (in these cases, the overall theme of a chapter) and a mental picture is built up of an entire thought structure.

Making your Mind Maps memorable

You have been shown how the mind thinks radiantly and works in a multidimensional nature. It follows, therefore, that notes which are themselves more 'holographic' and creative will be far more readily understood, appreciated and recalled than notes in the traditional linear format. That said, there are many devices we can use to make our note taking and note making Mind Maps even *more* memorable.

Arrows

These can be used to show how concepts that appear in different parts of a pattern are connected. The arrow can be single or multi-headed and can show backwards and forwards directions.

Codes

Asterisks, exclamation marks, crosses and question marks, as well as many other indicators, can be used next to words to show connections or other 'dimensions'.

The essential 'mind tools' for great brains

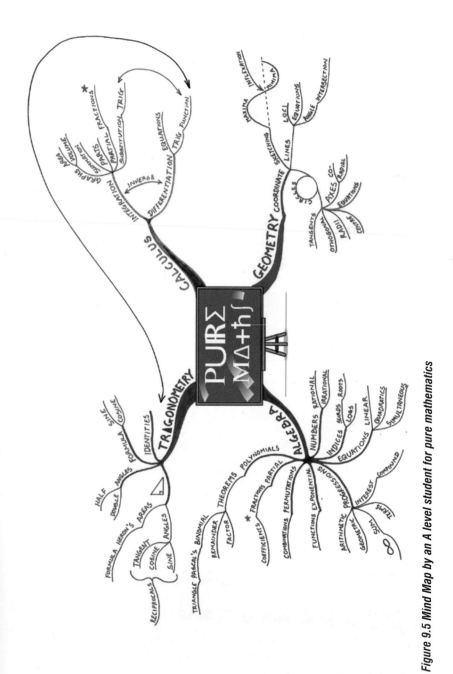

Figure 9.5 Mind Map by an A level student for pure mathematics

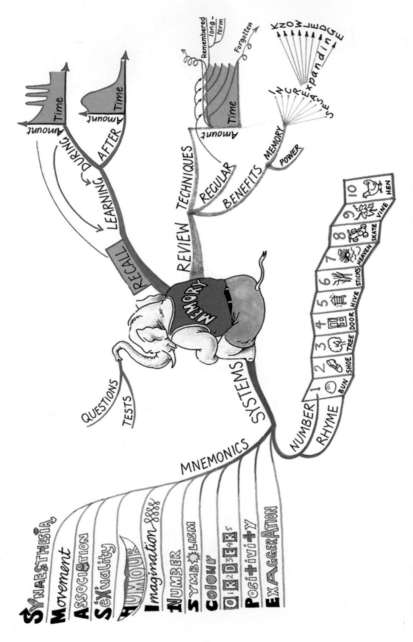

Figure 9.6 Mind Map of Chapters 4 and 5. 'Synaesthesia' (or sensuality) refers to the blending of the senses

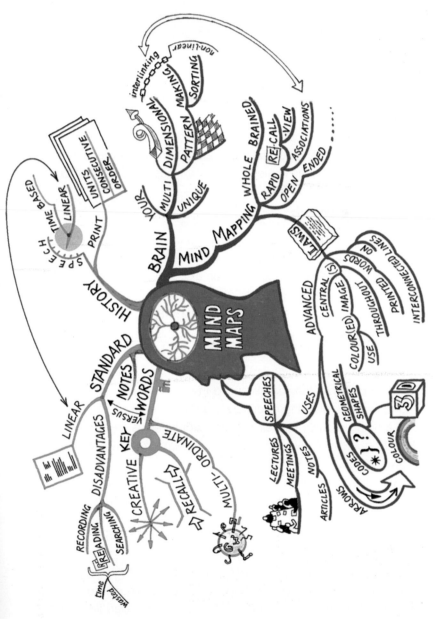

Figure 9.7 Mind Map of Chapters 7 and 8

Geometrical shapes

Squares, rectangles, circles, ellipses, and so on can be used to mark areas or words that are similar in nature. For example, triangles might be used to show areas of possible solution in a problem-solving pattern. Geometrical shapes can also be used to show order of importance.

Artistic three-dimensionality

Each of the geometrical shapes mentioned, and many others, can be given perspective. For example, a square can be made into a cube. The ideas printed in these shapes will thus, literally, stand out.

Even more colour

Colour is essential as a memory and creative aid. It can be used, like arrows, to show how concepts which appear in different parts of the Mind Map are connected. It can also be used to mark off the boundaries between major areas of a Mind Map.

Uses for Mind Maps

The nature of Mind Maps is intimately connected with how your mind functions so they can be used in nearly every activity where thought, recall, planning or creativity are involved (see Figure 9.8). For a detailed guide to their practical applications, see *The Mind Map Book* (BBC Active, 2010) and *Mind Maps for Business* (BBC Active, 2010).

Mind Maps are an external 'photograph' of the complex interrelationships between your thoughts at any given time. They enable your brain to 'see itself' more clearly and greatly enhance the full range of your thinking skills, increasing the levels of competence, enjoyment, elegance and fun in your life.

Today, we also have Mind Map computer software that can mimic hand-drawn techniques and make the technique virtually limitless in terms of its uses and applications. It is called iMindMap (see **www.thinkbuzan.com**) and follows the core laws and principles of Mind Mapping set out above. It allows you to create Mind

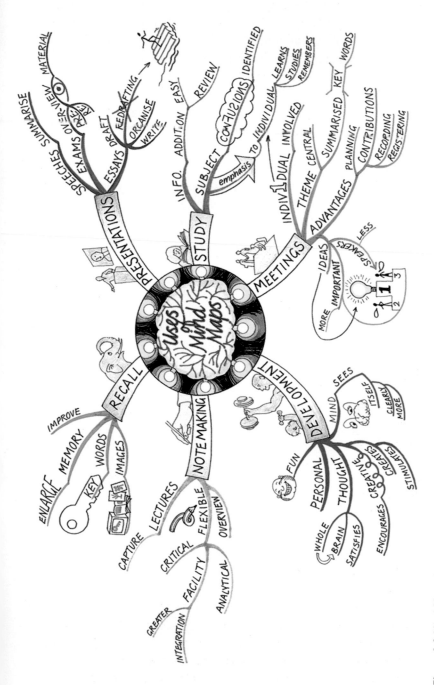

Figure 9.8 Mind Map of the uses of Mind Maps

Maps organically on screen and make corrections and amendments, as well as link your Mind Maps to other popular software applications. iMindMap is therefore particularly useful in government, business and educational environments for meetings, project management, planning and strategy and presentations (see also *Mind Maps for Business*, BBC Active, 2010).

As you learn to harness your memory and practise creating Mind Maps, you can begin to speed up your reading and comprehension skills, as well as focus on the broader problem-solving approach to managing information – be it absorbing, storing, recalling, retrieving, analysing, strategising, outputting or presenting – and getting all that learning within your super biocomputer, your brain, out into the world of study, work and self-improvement.

Speed read to save days, weeks, even months of your time

Speed reading is an absolute requirement for processing information in this age of 'information overload' and a core skill for more efficient learning.

In this chapter, you will learn that most of the beliefs you had about reading are wrong; you will find out how to deal with your major reading problems; and how to understand and use techniques that will double your reading speed while maintaining and/or improving your comprehension.

Reading problems

In the space overleaf, create a Mind Map of all the problems you have with reading and learning. Be strict with yourself. The more you are able to define, the more completely you will be able to improve.

Your own problems with reading and learning

The essential 'mind tools' for great brains

Teachers have noted over the past 20 years that, in each of their classes, the same general reading problems arise. Below is a list of those most commonly experienced. You are advised to check your own against these, adding any of them that apply to you – there will probably be quite a few.

- vision
- speed
- comprehension
- time
- amount
- note making
- retention

- fear
- fatigue
- boredom
- analysis
- organisation
- regression
- recall.

- vocabulary
- subvocalisation
- selection
- rejection
- concentration
- back skipping

Each of the problems listed above is serious and can, by itself, disrupt reading and learning. This book is devoted to solving those problems, and this chapter is concerned primarily with vision, speed, comprehension and the learning environment.

Before getting down to the more physical aspects of reading, I shall first define the term, then, in the light of that definition, explain why the wide range of problems that exist are so universally experienced.

What *is* reading really?

Reading, which is often defined as 'getting from the book what the author intended' or 'assimilating the written word', deserves a far more complete definition. It can be defined as the individual's total interrelationship with symbolic information. It is usually the visual aspect of learning and contains seven steps, as follows (see also Figure 10.1).

1 The first step is **recognition**. You have to be able to recognise the language and, whatever language you learn, it's the same process.

2 How do the symbols get in? By **assimilation**. This sounds straightforward but it is complex. It relates to your posture, health, general physical condition and, primarily, your eyes and how your brain uses them. You need to know how your eyes function and what actually goes on in order to work them, yet nobody is taught this. Assimilation is all about how you get that information into your head – and that is where all the facets of speed reading come in to play.

3 Next comes the need for **comprehension** – also called 'intra-integration' ('intra' meaning within, to itself) or connecting bits of information – the interconnections between the pieces of information within.

4 **Understanding** is different from comprehension. Once you have comprehended, then you can integrate that information with the outside world – that is, 'extra-integration', connecting the book to the outside universe. It is very different from step 3 (which is getting the book totally connected to *itself* in your head). This step involves getting the book completely related to your *other areas of knowledge*.

5 Now we have to learn how to memorise the information. Memory is quite a precise term in the definition of reading, referring to the two main factors in memory. First, **retention** – that is, storing the information in your brain's database, archive and library.

6 The second factor in memory is **recall**, which is the ability to hook out of your library the information stored there. Most people confuse this subdivision of memory with memory itself. For this reason, they are often heard saying, 'I have a terrible memory'. They actually have a superb memory, it's just that it is all stored and they can't get it out!

7 Why recall? Why read in the first place? For the purpose of **communication**. You want to apply the knowledge that you have acquired – to think about it, create from it, learn from it and build on it for lifelong future learning.

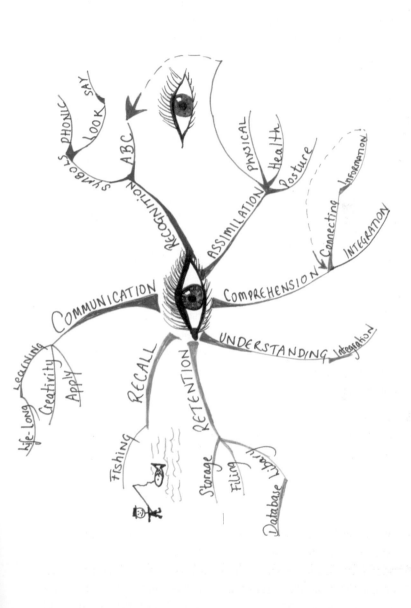

Figure 10.1 Mind Map of the seven major steps a fully mentally literate reader goes through and needs to master. This is a radically new definition of reading

The definition includes consideration of many of the problems listed at the start of this chapter. The only problems not included are those that are, in a sense, 'outside' the reading process, such as the influence of our reaction to our surroundings, time of day, energy level, interest, motivation, age and wellness.

Why reading problems exist

You may justifiably ask at this point why so many people experience typically common reading problems.

The answer, in addition to our previous lack of knowledge about the brain, lies in our approach to the initial teaching of reading. You and most of the other people reading this book, if you are over 25, will probably have been taught using the 'phonic' or 'alphabet' method. If not, you will probably have been taught by the 'look and say' method.

The most simplified phonic method teaches children the alphabet first, then the different sounds for each of the letters in the alphabet, the blending of sounds in syllables and, finally, the blending of sounds forming words. From this point on, they are given progressively more difficult books, usually in the form of graded series of stories, through which they progress at their own speed. They become 'silent' readers during that process.

The look and say methods teach children by presenting them with cards on which there are pictures. The names of the objects shown are clearly printed underneath them. Once the children have become familiar with the pictures and the names associated with them, the pictures are removed, leaving only the words. When the children have built up enough basic vocabulary, they progress through a series of graded books, similar to those given to children taught by the phonic method, and they also become 'silent' readers.

These outlines of the two methods are necessarily brief and there are at least 50 other methods similar to these presently being used in English-speaking countries. Similar problems exist all over the world.

The point about these methods, however, is that they are inadequate for teaching any child to read, in the complete sense of the word.

Referring to the seven steps to reading that I gave earlier, it can be seen that these methods are designed to cover only the *recognition* step in the process, with some attempt at *assimilation* and *comprehension*. The methods do not touch on the problems of speed, time, amount, retention, recall, selection, rejection, note making, concentration, appreciation, criticism, analysis, organisation, motivation, interest, boredom, surroundings, fatigue or typographic size and style – to name just a few!

It is perhaps not so surprising, therefore, that these problems are so widely experienced.

Recognition, it is important to note, is hardly ever mentioned as a problem, because it has been taught separately in the early years at school. All the other problems are mentioned because they have *not* been dealt with during the educational process. The next two chapters deal with the majority of these reading problems, while the remainder of this one is devoted to eye movements, comprehension and the speed of your reading.

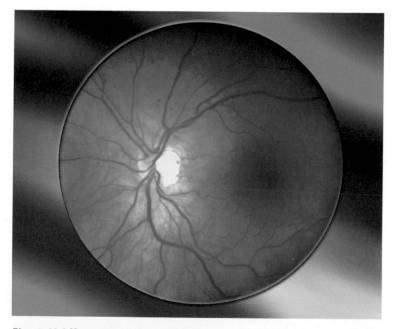

Figure 10.2 Your eye: a miracle of nature
Source: POD/Jupiter Images. Brand X. Alamy

Eye movements and reading

When asked to show with their forefingers the movement and speed of their eyes as they read, most people move their fingers along in smooth lines from left to right, with a quick jump from the end of one line back to the beginning of the next (see Figure 10.3). They normally take between a quarter and one second for each line.

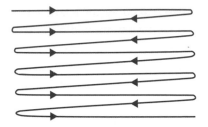

Figure 10.3 Assumed movement of the eyes while reading reported by people with no knowledge of eye movements. Each line is thought to be covered in less than one second

Two major errors are being made.

Speed

Even if your eyes moved as slowly as a line per second, words would be covered at the rate of 600–700 words per minute (wpm). As the average reading speed for even light material is 200 wpm, it can be seen that even those estimating slower speeds assume that they read words much more rapidly than they really do.

Movement

If eyes moved over print in the smooth manner shown in Figure 10.3, they would be able to take in nothing, because they can see things clearly only when they can 'hold them still'. If an object is still, the eyes must be still in order to see it and, if an object is moving, the eyes must move *with* the object in order to see it. A simple experiment that you can do, either by yourself or with a friend, will confirm this.

Hold a forefinger motionless in front of your eyes and either feel your own eyes or watch your friend's eyes as they look at the finger.

They will remain still. Next, move the finger up, down, sideways and around, following it with the eyes. Finally, move the finger up, down and around, holding the eyes still, or cross both hands in front of your face, at the same time looking at them both simultaneously. (If you can accomplish this last feat, write to me immediately!)

It will now be clear that when objects move, eyes move with them if they are to be seen clearly.

Relating all this to reading, it is obvious that, if your eyes are going to take in words and the words are still, your eyes will have to pause on each word before moving on. Rather than moving in the smooth lines shown in Figure 10.3, your eyes, in fact, move in a series of stops – called *fixations* – and quick jumps (see Figure 10.4).

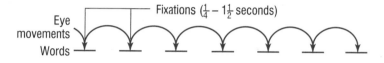

Figure 10.4 Diagram representing the stop and start movement of your eyes during the reading process

The jumps themselves are so quick as to take almost no time and the fixations can take anywhere from a ¼ to 1½ seconds. People who normally read one word at a time and skip back over words and letters are forced, by the simple mathematics of their eye movements, to read at speeds that are often well below 100 wpm, which means that they will not be able to understand much of what they read, nor be able to read much (see Figure 10.5).

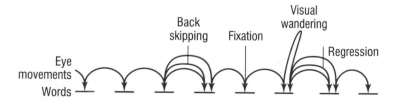

Figure 10.5 Diagram showing the poor reading habits of a slow reader – one word is read at a time, with unconscious back skipping, visual wandering and conscious regressions

It might seem at first glance that slow readers are doomed, but the problem can be solved, and in more than one way.

Speeding up

Happily there are many ways in which slow readers can accelerate their reading speeds and they are easy to do.

- Skipping back over words can be eliminated, as 90 per cent of back skipping and regression (the process of going back over and over a word) is based on apprehension and is unnecessary for understanding. The 10 per cent of words that do need to be reconsidered can be noted in Mind Map form or intelligently guessed, marked and looked up later.

- The time taken for each fixation can be reduced to approach the ¼-second minimum – you need not fear that this is too short a time, for your eyes are able to register as many as five words in one one-hundredth of a second.

- The size of the fixation can be expanded to take in as many as three to five words at a time (see Figure 10.6).

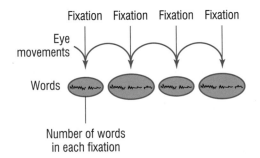

Figure 10.6 **Diagram showing the eye movements of a better and more effi-cient reader. More words are taken in at each fixation, and back skipping, regression and visual wandering are reduced**

This solution might at first seem impossible if it is true that your mind deals with one word at a time. In fact, it can equally well fixate on *groups* of words, which is better in nearly all ways. That is because, when you read a sentence, you do not read it for the

The essential 'mind tools' for great brains

individual meaning of each word, you read it for the meaning of the phrases in which the words are contained.

For example, reading: the   cat
                    sat   on   the
road is more difficult than reading: the cat sat   on the road.

Slower readers have to do more mental work than faster, smoother readers because they have to add the meaning of each word to the meaning of each following word. In the above example, that amounts to five or six additions. More efficient readers absorb in meaningful units so have only one simple addition to make.

The advantages of reading faster

If you are a faster reader, your eyes will be doing less physical work on each page. Rather than having as many as 500 fixations tightly focused per page that a slow reader would do, you will have as few as 100 fixations per page, each of which is less muscularly fatiguing as it does not last as long as that of a slower reader.

Another advantage is that the rhythm and flow of faster reading will carry you comfortably through the meaning, whereas a slower reader, because of the stopping and starting, jerky pattern, will be far more likely to become bored, lose concentration, drift away mentally and lose the meaning of what is being read.

Common assumptions about reading

From all that we have read above, we can conclude that a number of commonly held beliefs about faster readers turn out to be false, such as the following.

- 'Words must be read one at a time.' Wrong – because of your ability to fixate and because you read for meaning rather than for single words.

- 'Reading faster than 500 wpm is impossible.' Wrong – because the fact that you can take in as many as six words per fixation and make four fixations a second means speeds of 1000 wpm are perfectly feasible.

- 'A faster reader is not able to appreciate.' Wrong – because a faster reader will understand more of the meaning of what is being read, concentrate on the material more and have considerably more time to go back over areas of special interest and importance.

- 'Higher speeds mean lower levels of concentration.' Wrong – because the faster you go, the more impetus you gather and the more you concentrate.

- 'Average reading speeds are natural and therefore the best.' Wrong – because average reading speeds are *not* natural. They are speeds produced by an incomplete initial training in reading, combined with an inadequate knowledge of how your eyes and brain work at the various speeds possible.

The next chapter includes exercises and tests to develop your reading skills. The best way to practise these is on a licensed Buzan speed reading course (see Appendix).

The incredible power of 'super' speed reading

When children learn how to read, they often point with their finger to the words they are reading. Adults have traditionally regarded this as a fault and have told children to take their fingers off the page. It is now realised that it is the adults, not the children, who are at fault. Instead of insisting that they move their fingers, adults should simply ask children to move their fingers faster. It is obvious that the finger does not slow down the eyes and the added values that the aid gives in establishing a smooth, rhythmical habit are immeasurable.

To observe the difference between unaided and aided eye movements, ask a friend to imagine a large circle about 30 cm (1ft) in front of them, then ask them to look slowly and carefully around the circumference. Rather than move in a perfect circle, your friend's eyes will follow a pattern more like an arthritic rectangle (see Figure 11.1).

Next, trace a circle in the air with your finger, asking your friend to follow the tip of your finger with their eyes as you move smoothly around the circumference. You will observe that your friend's eyes follow your finger almost perfectly and trace a circle similar to that shown in Figure 11.2.

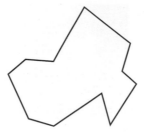

Figure 11.1 The pattern made by eyes attempting to move around the circumference of a circle unaided

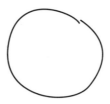

Figure 11.2 The pattern made by eyes moving around the circumference of a circle when aided

This simple experiment indicates what an enormous improvement in performance there can be if a person is given the basic information about the physical functioning of the eyes and brain. In many instances no long training or arduous practising is necessary. The results, as in this case, are immediate.

You need not be restricted to using your index finger as a visual aid – you can use to advantage a pen or a pencil, as many naturally efficient readers do. At first, the visual aid will make your reading speed look slow. That is because, as mentioned earlier, we all imagine we read a lot faster than we actually do, but your aided reading speed will actually be faster.

The essential 'mind tools' for great brains

Expand your focus

This exercise is designed to expand your visual power so that you are able to take in more words 'at a glance' when you look at a page than before.

Read through the instructions once first before trying the technique or, alternatively, ask someone to read the instructions to you while you follow the directions.

1 Look straight ahead and focus your attention on a point on the horizon as far away as possible.
2 Touch the tips of your two index fingers together so that they form a horizontal line, then hold them approximately 10 cm (4 in) in front of your nose.
3 While keeping your eyes fixed on your chosen point in the distance, begin to wiggle the tips of your fingers and move them apart slowly, along a straight, horizontal line. (You will need to move your arms and elbows apart as well, but keep the movement horizontal.)
4 Keep going until your fingers move just outside your field of vision and you can no longer see the movement of your fingers out of the corners of your eyes.
5 Stop and ask your friend to measure how far apart your fingers are (Figure 11.3).

Figure 11.3 Moving your fingers apart to find extent of field of vision

6 Now repeat the exercise, but with one finger pointing upwards and the other downwards, so that your fingertips meet and form a vertical line this time. Again, hold them together, approximately 10 cm (4 in) in front of your nose.

7 While keeping your eyes fixed firmly on your chosen point in the distance as before, begin to wiggle your fingers and move them apart – one upwards, one downwards – in a vertical line so that they gradually move out of the top and bottom of your field of vision.

8 Stop and ask your friend to measure how far apart your fingers are (see Figure 11.3).

Does it surprise you to find out just how much and how far you can see when you are apparently focused solely on something else? How is that possible?

The reason for this lies in the unique design of the human eye. Each of your eyes has 130 million light receivers in its retina, which means that you have 260 million receivers of light in total. Your central focus (the part you use to read your book or focus on the point in the distance) takes up only 20 per cent of that light-receiving capacity. The rest – that is, 80 per cent of the total light receivers – are devoted to your peripheral vision.

By learning to make greater use of your peripheral vision while you are reading, you will begin to utilise its vast untapped potential – that of your mind's eye. What do I mean by your 'mind's eye'? I mean the ability to read or see with your *entire* brain, not just with your eyes. It is a concept that is recognised by those who practise yoga, meditation, prayer and anyone familiar with learning to 'see' Magic Eye™ three-dimensional pictures.

High speed perception

Choose a book and simply turn the pages as fast as possible, attempting to see as many words per page as possible.

This form of training will increase your ability to take in large groups of words per fixation, improve your overviewing and previewing techniques and condition your mind to much more rapid and efficient general reading practices.

This high-speed conditioning can be compared to driving along a continental motorway at 90 mph for an hour. Imagine you had been driving at that speed and suddenly came to a road sign saying '30'. To what speed would you slow down if somebody covered your speedometer and said 'go on, tell me when you reach 30'. The answer of course would be 50 to 60 mph (see Figure 11.4).

The reason for this is that your mind has become conditioned to the much higher speed, which becomes 'normal'. Previous 'normals' are more or less forgotten in the presence of the new ones. The same applies to reading and, after practising at high speed you will often find yourself reading at twice your normal speed without even feeling the difference.

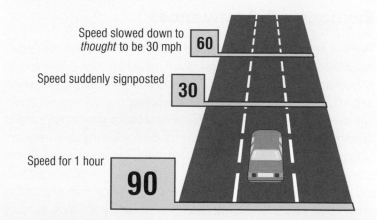

Speed slowed down to *thought* to be 30 mph **60**

Speed suddenly signposted **30**

Speed for 1 hour **90**

Figure 11.4 Illustration of how the mind 'gets used to' speed and motion. The same kind of relativistic 'misjudgements' can be used to your advantage to help you learn to learn more effectively

Motivational practice

Most reading is done at a relaxed, almost lackadaisical pace – a fact that many speed reading courses have taken advantage of. Students are given various exercises and tasks and it is suggested to them that, after each exercise, their speed will increase by 10 to 20 wpm. So it does, often by as much as 100 per cent by the end of the course. That increase, however, is often due not to the exercises but the fact that the student's motivation has been increased bit by bit during the course.

The same significant increases could be produced by guaranteeing each student, at the beginning of the course, the fulfilment of any wish he or she desires. Performance would immediately equal that normally achieved at the end of such courses – rather like the unathletic person who runs a 100-metre dash and jumps a high fence when being chased by a bull. In these cases motivation is the major factor and you will benefit enormously by consciously applying it to each learning experience. If a deep-rooted decision is made to do better, then your performance will automatically improve.

Environmental influences

There is no doubt that your internal physical posture and your external working or study environment will influence your propensity to concentrate and improve. This applies equally to memory training and Mind Mapping as well as speed reading.

So, if you are feeling negative or unwell, or your study area is crammed or cluttered, your state of being will have a negative influence on your productivity. If, however, you are happy in your environment and inwardly content, you will react positively to reading and comprehend new information. It therefore makes sense to ensure that your environment is as positive and conducive to study as possible.

Placement and intensity of light

Whenever possible, it is best to work or study in natural daylight. Indeed, a recent study found that exposing yourself to daylight allows

The essential 'mind tools' for great brains

your brain to release more 'feel-good' hormones, so your desk or tabletop should ideally be placed near a window. At other times, artificial light should come over your shoulder, opposite the hand with which you write. The lamp should be bright enough to illuminate the material being read, but not so bright that it provides a contrast with the rest of the room. If you are using a desktop or laptop computer, then the screen should be facing towards, not behind, the light.

Distance of the eyes from the reading material

The natural distance for your eyes from your reading material is approximately 50 cm (20 in). That makes it easier for your eyes to focus on groups of words and lessens the possibility of eye strain or headaches.

Your posture

Ideally, your feet should be flat on the floor, your back upright, with the slight curve at the base of your spine maintained to give you support. If you sit up either *too* straight or slumped, you will exhaust yourself and strain your back. Try either holding the book or resting it on something so that it is slightly upright rather than flat.

Sitting correctly has a number of physiological benefits for studying:

- your brain receives the maximum flow of air and blood because your windpipe, veins and arteries are unrestricted and can function properly

- it will optimise the flow of energy up your spine and maximise the power of your brain

- if your body is alert, then your brain knows that something important is happening (conversely, if you sit in a slumped position, you are telling your brain that it is time to sleep!)

- your eyes can make full use of both your central and peripheral vision.

Test your speed

To calculate your speed in words per minute, take the following steps.

1 Read for one minute – note your starting and stopping points.
2 Count the number of words on three lines.
3 Divide that number by three to give you the average number of words per line.
4 Count the total number of lines read (balancing short lines out).
5 Multiply the average number of words per line by the number of lines you read, which will equal your reading speed in words per minute (wpm).

The formula for working out speed in wpm is:

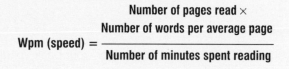

$$\text{Wpm (speed)} = \frac{\text{Number of pages read} \times \text{Number of words per average page}}{\text{Number of minutes spent reading}}$$

The graph below is provided for you if you wish to chart your speed reading progress.

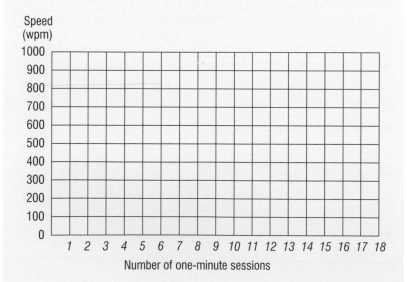

Number of one-minute sessions

Metronome training

A metronome, which is usually used for keeping a musical rhythm, can be most useful for both reading and high-speed reading practice.

If you set the metronome to a reasonable pace, each beat can indicate a single sweep of your eyes. In this way, a steady and smooth rhythm can be maintained and the usual slowdown that occurs after a little while can be avoided. Once the most comfortable rhythm has been found, your reading speed can be improved by occasionally adding an extra beat per minute.

A metronome can also be used to pace high-speed perception exercises. You can start at a slower rate and accelerate to exceptionally fast rates, eventually 'looking' at one page per beat.

The information you have picked up now on eye movements, visual aids and advanced reading techniques should be applied to each of your reading situations (if you are especially interested in pursuing the full range of speed and range reading skills, refer to *The Speed Reading Book*, BBC Active, 2010). You will find that these techniques and pieces of advice will become more useful when they are applied together with information and techniques from the other chapters.

The next chapter gives you the simple-to-follow, eight-point BOST strategy for study preparation and application. *Preparation* includes the key skills of browsing, time management, refreshing memory and defining questions and goals, while *application* is divided into overview, preview, inview and review skills.

12

Revolutionise your study skills with the Buzan Organic Study Technique (BOST)

The Buzan Organic Study Technique (BOST), laid out in this chapter, enables you to develop strong study habits and overcome those typical fears, stresses and anxieties that come with learning. The techniques set out here can be adapted to any subject – from business to biotechnology to Babylonian history.

First, you have to overcome those quite rational fears of exams, tests, assessments, essays, writing a thesis and coursework.

Most people experience difficulties in studying or revising. The key barriers to successful study are what I term 'the reluctant learner', 'the mental blocks to effective study' and 'outdated study techniques'.

The reluctant learner

The six-o'clock-in-the-evening-enthusiastic-determined-and-well-intentioned-studier-until-midnight person is someone with whom you are probably already familiar.

At 6 p.m. he (such a learner could equally be a she, but we'll make this one a he to avoid the repetitive 'he or she') approaches his desk and carefully organises everything in preparation for the study period to follow. Having everything in place, our reluctant learner next adjusts each item carefully again, giving him time to think of the first excuse not to work – he remembers that, in the morning, there was not quite enough time to browse the news as well as check his e-mails and blogs online. So, he decides that it is best to get these out of the way first before the serious research begins. Of course, it takes longer than originally anticipated and then there are items of interest in the newspaper that he'd scanned earlier but not had a chance to read. The rationalisation is that it is best to have these small items also completely out of the way before settling down to the task at hand.

Our learner therefore leaves his desk, browses through the newspaper and notices as he does so that there are more articles of interest than he had originally thought. He also notices, as he leafs through the pages, the entertainment section. At that point it seems like a good idea to plan for the evening's first break – perhaps an interesting half-hour TV programme between 8 and 8.30 p.m.

He finds an interesting programme and, inevitably, it starts at 7 p.m. At that point, he thinks 'Well, I've had a difficult day and it's not too long before the programme starts. I need a rest anyway and the relaxation will really help me to get down to studying ...' He returns to his desk at 7.45 p.m, because the beginning of the next programme was also a bit more interesting than he thought it would be.

At that stage, he still hovers over his desk, tapping his book reassuringly, when he remembers that phone call and text message to his two fellow students he had meant to do earlier. Just like the articles of interest in the newspaper, he thinks it would be best to get them out of the way before the serious studying begins.

The phone call and texts coming back and forth, of course, are much more interesting and take longer than originally planned, meaning that, eventually our intrepid studier finds himself back at his desk at about 8.30 p.m.

At that point in the proceedings, he actually sits down at his desk, opens the book with a display of physical determination and starts to read (usually page 1). He then experiences the first pangs of hunger and thirst. This is disastrous because he realises the longer he waits to satisfy the pangs, the worse they will get and the more interrupted his study concentration will be.

The obvious and only solution is a light snack, but, as more and more tasty items are added to placate his hunger, the snack becomes a feast.

Having removed this final obstacle, our learner returns to his desk with the certain knowledge that this time there is nothing that could possibly interfere with him studying. The first couple of sentences on page 1 are looked at again ... He realises that his stomach is feeling decidedly heavy and a general drowsiness seems to have set in. Far better at this juncture to watch that *other* interesting half-hour programme at 10 p.m., after he will have digested and the rest will enable him to really get down to the task at hand.

At midnight, we find him asleep in front of the TV.

Even at this point, when he has been woken up by whoever comes into the room, he will think that things have not gone too badly, for, after all, he has had a good rest, a good meal, watched some interesting and relaxing programmes, fulfilled his social commitments to his friends, caught up with the paper and got everything completely out of the way so that *tomorrow* at 6 p.m. ...

What we can learn from this little scenario is that information is being given more importance and emphasis than the individual. As a result he is being mentally swamped and almost literally weighed down by it all (see Figure 12.1). In today's world, both the information and publication explosions are still continuing at staggering rates, while the ability of the individual to handle and study it all remains neglected. If our learner is ever to cope with the situation, he must learn not more 'hard facts' but new ways of handling and studying the information – new ways to use his natural abilities to learn, think, recall, create and find solutions to problems.

Figure 12.1 Fear of coming to grips with study is a rational fear based on pure logic, as we live in an age of information explosion

The mental blocks to effective study

The preceding episode is probably familiar and amusing, but the implications of it are significant and serious.

On one level the story is encouraging because, by the very fact that it is a problem experienced by everybody, it confirms what has long been suspected: that everyone is creative and inventive and the feelings many have about being uncreative are mistaken. The creativity demonstrated in the example of the reluctant student is not applied very usefully, but the diversity and originality with which we all make up infinite number of reasons for *not* doing things suggests each person has a wealth of talent that could be applied in much more positive directions.

On another level, the story is discouraging because it shows up the widespread and underlying fear that most of us experience when confronted with a study text.

That reluctance and fear arises from the examination-based education system, in which students are presented with textbooks on the subjects they are 'taking'. They know that textbooks are 'harder' than storybooks and novels; they also know that they represent a lot of work; and, further, they knows they will be tested on their knowledge of the information in the books. As a result:

- the fact that this type of book is 'hard' is discouraging in itself

- the fact that the books represent work is also discouraging, because students instinctively 'know' that they are unable to read, note and remember properly

- the fact that they are going to be tested is often the most serious of the three difficulties.

It is well known that this last threat can completely disrupt your brain's ability to work in certain situations. The number of cases are legion of people who literally cannot write anything in an exam situation, despite the fact that they know their subjects thoroughly. There are also many people who, even though they are able to write some form of answer, have gigantic mental blocks so whole areas of knowledge are completely forgotten during an exam period. In even more extreme cases, many people have been known to spend a whole two-hour period writing frantically, assuming that they are answering the question, but, in fact, repeating over and over again either their own name or one word.

Faced with this kind of threat, which for many is truly terrifying, students have one of two choices: they can either study and face one set of consequences or not study and face a different set of consequences. If they study and do badly, then they 'prove' that they are 'incapable', 'unintelligent', 'stupid', a 'dunce' or some other negative expression. Of course, that is not really the case, but they have no way of knowing that it is the *system* not testing them properly, not their own ineptitude, that is causing the 'failure'.

If they do not study, the situation is quite different. Confronted with having failed a test or exam, they can immediately say that of course they failed it because they didn't study and weren't interested in that kind of stuff anyway.

By doing this, the reluctant student solves the above problem in a number of ways:

- he avoids both the test and the threat to his self-esteem that studying would involve

- he has a perfect excuse for failing

- he gains the respect of fellow students because he is daring to attack a situation that is frightening to them as well.

It is interesting to note that such a student will often find himself in the position of a leader.

It is also interesting to note that even those who do make the decision to study will still reserve a little part of themselves that behaves like the student who doesn't study. Those achieving marks as high as 80 or 90 per cent will still also be found using exactly the same excuses for not getting 100 per cent that the student who doesn't study uses for failing.

Outdated study techniques

The situations described are unsatisfactory for everyone concerned. One further and major reason for poor study results lies in the way that we tend to approach both study techniques and the information we want people to study.

We have surrounded students with a confusing mass of different subjects or 'disciplines', demanding that they learn, remember and understand a frightening array of material under headings such as mathematics, physics, chemistry, biology, zoology, botany, anatomy, physiology, sociology, psychology, anthropology, philosophy, history, geography, English, media studies, music technology, palaeontology and so on (see Figure 12.2). In each of these subject areas, individuals have been and are still presented with series of dates, theories, facts, names and general ideas.

What this really means is that we have been taking a totally lopsided approach to study and the way in which students deal with and relate to the information and knowledge that surround them. We concentrate far too much on information about the 'separate' areas of knowledge. We also lay too much stress on asking individuals to feed back facts in a predigested order or preset forms, such as standard examination papers or formal essays.

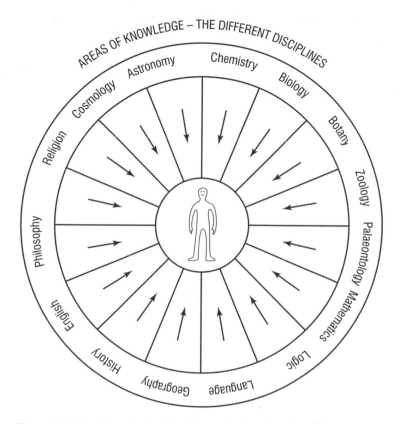

Figure 12.2 In traditional education, information is given or taught about the different areas of knowledge that surround the individual. The direction and flow is from the subject to the individual – the student is simply given the information and expected to absorb, learn and remember as much as possible

This approach has also been reflected in the standard study techniques recommended in sixth-form colleges, universities, institutes of further education and the textbooks and other study aids that go with them. These techniques are 'grid' approaches in which it is recommended that a series of steps be worked through for any book being studied. One common suggestion is that any reasonably difficult study book should always be read through three times in order to ensure a complete understanding. Even the many more developed approaches tend to be comparatively rigid and, inflexible – simply standard systems, to be repeated each time we study.

It is obvious that methods such as these cannot be applied with success to every study book. There is an enormous difference between studying a text on literary criticism and one on higher mathematics. In order to study properly, a technique is needed that does not force the same approach to be used for such different materials.

First, it is necessary to start working from the individual outwards. Rather than bombarding students with books, formulae and examinations, we must begin to concentrate on teaching each person how he or she can study most efficiently. We must teach ourselves how our eyes work when we read, how we remember, how we think, how we can learn more effectively, how we can organise our notes, how we can solve problems and, in general, how we can best use our abilities, whatever the subject matter (see Figure 12.3).

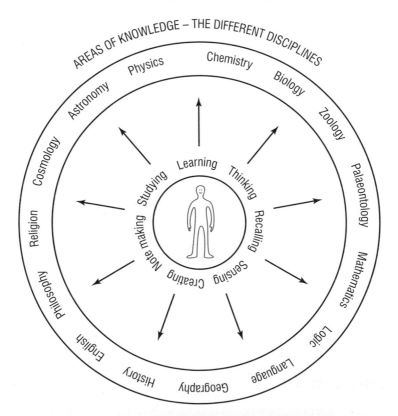

Figure 12.3 In the new forms of education, the previous emphases must be reversed. Instead of first teaching students facts about other things, we must first teach them facts about themselves – facts about how they can learn, think, recall, create, solve problems and so on

The essential 'mind tools' for great brains

Most of the problems outlined here will be eliminated when we finally shift the emphasis away from the subjects and towards the students and show how they can each select and understand any information that they want to. Students will be equipped to study and remember whatever area of knowledge is interesting or necessary. Things will not have to be taught to them or 'crammed in'. Students will be able to range subjects at their own pace, going for help and personal supervision only when they realise that it is necessary. Yet another advantage of this approach is that it will make both teaching and learning much easier, more enjoyable and more productive. By concentrating on individuals and their abilities, we will finally and sensibly have placed the learning situation in its proper perspective – which brings us on to BOST.

BOST

BOST (Buzan Organic Study Technique) is based on the premise that you need to learn how to learn *before* you learn any particular subject.

It is divided into two main strategies:

1 *Preparation*, itself divided into browse, time and amount, five-minute jotter, and asking questions and defining goals.

2 *Application*, broken down into the four strategies of overview, preview, inview and review.

It is important to note at the outset that, although the main steps are presented in a certain order, that order is by no means essential and can be changed, subtracted from and added to as the study or preparation warrant. You will also need to read and revisit Chapters 5, 9 and 10 – on memory Mind Maps and speed reading, respectively – to utilise the BOST programme to maximum effect.

Preparation

This first part of the programme consists of the following steps:

- browse

- time and amount

- five-minute jotter

- asking questions and defining goals.

Browse

Before doing anything else, it is essential to 'browse' – that is, look through the entire textbook, journal, lecture notes or whatever it is that you are about to study.

Your browse should be done in the same way that you would look through a book you were considering buying in a bookshop or taking out from a library. In other words, casually and rather rapidly, flipping through the pages, getting the general 'feel' of the book, observing the organisation and structure, the level of difficulty, proportion of diagrams and illustrations to text, location of any results, and summaries and conclusions.

Time and amount

These two aspects can be dealt with simultaneously because the theory behind them both is similar.

The first thing to do when sitting down to study a textbook is decide on the period of time to be devoted to it. Having done that, decide what amount to cover in the time allocated.

The reason for insisting on these two initial steps is not arbitrary, and is supported by the findings of Gestalt psychologists ('Gestalt' means 'completing tendency'). To test this yourself, do Exercise 16.

The Gestalt psychologists discovered that the human brain has a very strong tendency to complete things. Thus most people will label the shapes in Exercise 16 straight line, cylinder, square, ellipse or oval, zigzag line, circle, triangle, wavy or curved line and rectangle. In fact, the 'circle' is not a circle but a 'broken circle'. Many actually see the broken circle as a circle. Others see it as a broken circle, but assume that the artist intended to complete it.

When we are studying, making a decision about the aspects of time and amount – what we want to complete – gives us a secure anchor, as well as an end point or goal. It has the added advantage of enabling the proper linkages to be made, rather than encouraging us to wander off in more disconnected ways.

Shape recognition

Enter the names of the shapes of each of the items in the spaces provided.

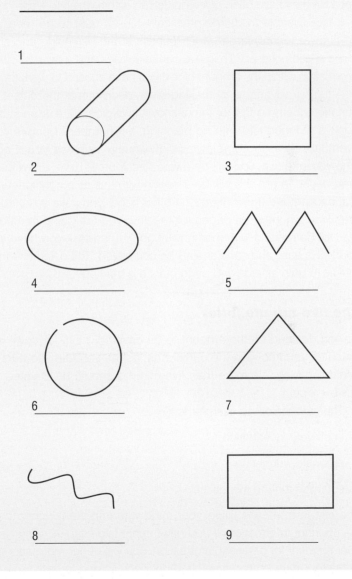

1 _____

2 _____

3 _____

4 _____

5 _____

6 _____

7 _____

8 _____

9 _____

An excellent comparison is that of listening to a good lecturer. The lecturer, attempting to expound a lot of difficult material, will usually explain his or her starting and ending points and will often indicate the amount of time to be spent on each area of the presentation. The audience will automatically find the lecture easy to follow because they have been given guidelines within which to work.

It is advisable to define physically the amount to be read by placing reasonably large paper markers at the beginning and end of the section chosen. Then you can refer back and forwards to the information within the amount of text you have chosen to work on.

A further advantage of making these decisions at the outset is that the underlying fear of the unknown is avoided. If a large study book is plunged into with no planning, the number of pages you eventually have to complete will continually oppress you. Each time you sit down, you will be aware that you still have 'a few hundred pages to go' and will be studying with this as a constant and real background threat. If, on the other hand, you have selected a reasonable number of pages for the time you are going to study, you will be reading with the knowledge that the task you have set yourself is easy and can certainly be completed. The difference this makes to both attitude and performance is marked.

The five-minute jotter

Having decided on the amount to be covered, next, jot down as much as you know on the subject as fast as you can. Do it as a mini-Mind Map. No more than five minutes should be devoted to this exercise.

The purpose of this exercise is to:

- improve concentration

- eliminate wandering

- establish a good mental 'set'.

The last term means filling your mind with important rather than unimportant information. If you have spent five minutes searching your memory for pertinent information, you will be far more attuned to the text material than if you had not done so and far less likely to

The essential 'mind tools' for great brains

continue thinking about the strawberries and cream you are going to eat afterwards or whatever else you might be doing.

The time limit of five minutes for this exercise makes it clear that your entire knowledge is not required – it is intended purely to activate your storage system and set your mind off in the right direction.

One question that will arise is, What if I know almost nothing on the subject or if I know an enormous amount?'

If your knowledge of the area is *great*, the five minutes should be spent recalling the *major* divisions, theories, names and so on connected with the subject. As your mind can flash through information much faster than your hand can write it down, all the minor associations will still be 'seen' mentally and the proper mental set and direction will be established.

If your knowledge of the subject is almost *non-existent*, the five minutes should be spent recalling those few things you *do* know, as well as any other information that seems in any way at all connected. That will enable you to get as close as you possibly can to the new subject and prevent you from feeling totally lost, as so many do in such a situation.

The five-minute jotter has the very positive benefit of enabling to gather together your immediate and current state of knowledge on areas of interest. In that way, you will be able to keep much more up to date with yourself and will actually *know what you know*, rather than being in a continually embarrassing position of *not* knowing what you know – the 'I've got it on the tip of my tongue' syndrome.

Asking questions and defining goals

Having established your current state of knowledge on a subject, next decide what you want from the book. That involves defining the questions you want answered during your reading. Those questions should refer directly to what you wish to achieve. Many people like to use a different-coloured pen for this section and add their questions to a Mind Map jotting of current knowledge.

This exercise, like that for noting knowledge, is based on the principle of establishing proper mental sets. It should also take not much more than five minutes at the outset, as questions can be redefined and added to as the reading progresses.

A standard experiment to confirm this approach takes two groups of people who are generally equal in terms of age, education and aptitude. Each group is given the same study text and is given enough time to complete the whole book.

Those in Group A are told that they are going to be given a completely comprehensive test on everything in the book and must study accordingly.

Those in Group B are told that they will be tested on two or three major themes that run through the book and also must study accordingly.

Both groups are then, in fact, tested on the entire text, a situation that you would immediately think unfair to those in the group that had been told they would be tested only on the main themes.

You might also think that, in this situation, those in the second group would do better on questions about the themes they had been given, those in the first group better on other questions and both groups might have a similar final score. To the surprise of many, those in the second group not only did better on questions about the themes but also achieved higher total scores, which included better marks for *all* parts of the test.

The reason for that is the main themes act like great grappling hooks through the information, attaching everything else to them. In other words, the main questions and goals acted as associative and linking centres, to which all other information became easily attached.

Those in the group instructed to learn everything had no centres at all to connect new information to and, because of that, were groping, with no foundations, through the information. It is much like a situation in which people are given so much choice that they end up making no decision – the paradox of attempting to get everything and gaining nothing.

Asking questions and establishing goals can be seen, like the step preceding it, to become more and more important as the theory behind them becomes better understood. It should be emphasised that the more accurately those questions and goals are established, the better you will perform in the next part of BOST: application.

Application

This second part of the programme is broken down into the following steps:

- overview
- preview
- inview
- review.

Overview

One of the interesting facts about people using study books or course texts is that most, when given a new text, start reading on page 1. It is not advisable to start reading a new study text on the first page. Here's why.

Imagine that you are fanatical about doing jigsaw puzzles. A friend arrives on your doorstep with a gigantic box wrapped in paper, tied with string, and tells you that it's a present, saying, 'It's the most beautiful and complex jigsaw puzzle yet devised by man!' You thank her and, as you watch her walk away down the front path, you decide that, from that moment on, you are going to devote yourself entirely to the completion of the puzzle.

Before continuing, note in precise detail the steps that you would take from that point on in order to complete the task.

_____

_____

_____

_____

_____

_____

_____

_____

_____

_____

_____

Now check your own answers with those in the following list compiled from those my students gave.

1   Go back inside the house.

2   Take the string off the box.

3   Take off the paper.

4   Dispose of string and paper.

5   Look at the picture on the outside of the box.

6   Read the instructions, concentrating on the number of pieces and overall dimensions of the puzzle.

7   Estimate and organise the amount of time necessary for completion.

8   Plan breaks and meals!

9   Find a surface of appropriate dimensions for the puzzle.

10   Open the box.

11   Empty the contents of the box on to the surface or separate tray.

12   If pessimistic, check the number of pieces!

13   Turn all the pieces right side up.

14   Find the edge and corner pieces.

15   Sort out the colour areas.

16   Fit the 'obvious' bits and pieces together.

17   Continue to fill in.

18   Leave the 'difficult' pieces to the end (reasoning that, as the overall picture becomes clearer and the number of pieces used increases, so does the probability the difficult pieces will fit in much more easily as there is more of the context into which they can fit).

19   Continue the process until completion.

20   Celebrate!

This jigsaw story can be applied directly to study. Starting on page 1 is like finding the bottom left-hand corner-piece and insisting to yourself that the entire picture can be built up step by step from the corner only!

What is essential in a reasonable approach to study texts and course notes, especially difficult ones, is to get a good idea of what's in them before plodding on into a learning catastrophe.

The overview step in BOST is designed to perform this task and may be likened to looking at the picture, reading the instructions and finding the edge and corner pieces of the puzzle. What this means in the study context is that you should scour the book for all material not included in the regular body of the text, using your visual guide as you do so.

Areas of the book to be covered in your overview include:

- results
- summaries
- conclusions
- quotes or displayed text
- glossaries
- back cover

- tables
- table of contents
- margin notes
- illustrations
- capitalised words
- photographs

- subheadings
- dates
- italics
- graphs
- footnotes
- statistics.

The function of this process is to provide you with a good knowledge of the graphic sections of the book, and to ensure that you skim through the whole thing and select specific areas to cover relatively comprehensively (see Figure 12.4).

Amount of material to be studied

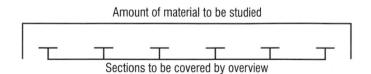

Sections to be covered by overview

Figure 12.4 Sections of a study text to be covered by overview (speed reading is a great aid here – see Chapter 10)

It is extremely important to note again that, throughout the overview, a pen, pencil or other form of visual guide should always be used. The reason for this can best be explained by reference to a graph (see Figure 12.5). If your eyes are unguided, they will simply fixate briefly on general areas of the graph, then move off, leaving only a vague visual memory and cause interference to that memory because the eye movement will not have 'registered' the same pattern as the graph (see Figure 12.6).

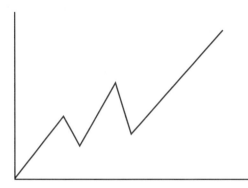

Figure 12.5 **Example of the pattern of a graph to be studied**

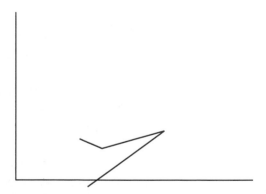

Figure 12.6 **Standard pattern formed when eyes following a graph are unguided, causing a conflicting memory of the shape of the graph**

The essential 'mind tools' for great brains

If a visual aid is used, your eyes will more nearly approximate the flow of the graph and your memory will be strengthened by each of the following inputs:

- the visual memory itself

- the remembered eye movements approximating the shape of the graph

- the memory of the movement of your arm or hand tracing the graph (kinaesthetic memory – see multiple intelligences, Chapter 3).

- the visual memory of the rhythm and movement of the tracer.

The overall recall resulting from this practice is far superior to that of a person who reads without using a visual guide. It is interesting to note that accountants often use their pens to guide their eyes across and down columns and rows of figures. They do so naturally because any very rigid linear eye movement is difficult to maintain with the unaided eye.

Preview

To preview something means just that: to pre-view, or, see before. If you allow your brain to see the whole text before speed reading it (by skimming, in association with one of the guided reading techniques), you will be able to navigate your way through it more effectively when you read it the second time.

The purpose of previewing material before reading it is the same as the purpose of planning a route before driving from A to B. You need to know the terrain and decide whether to take the long, scenic route or if a shortcut will suffice.

You should review everything that you are studying but also communications such as exam details and e-mails. If done effectively, it will save you an immense amount of time and speed up your levels of reading and comprehension.

Strategies for effective previewing include the following.

- Be aware of what you already know before you begin reading a book or a document and have an idea of what you want to achieve by reading it. Skim read the text first to discover the core elements. If the text is describing something you know already, make a note of the fact for future reference.

- Take effective notes on everything you read so that you can refer back to them in future and use your previously acquired knowledge to assess the relevance of what you are reading.

- During the preview, concentration should be directed to the beginnings and ends of paragraphs, sections, chapters and even whole texts, because information tends to be concentrated at the beginnings and ends of written material.

- If you are studying a short academic paper or a complex study book, the summary, results and conclusion sections should always be read first. Such sections often include exactly those concentrated essences of information that you are searching for, enabling you to grasp them without having to wade through a lot of time-wasting material.

- Having gained the essences from those sections, simply check that they do indeed summarise the main body of the text.

- In the preview, as with the overview, simply concentrate once again on the special areas (see Figure 12.7).

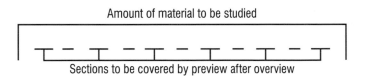

Amount of material to be studied

Sections to be covered by preview after overview

Figure 12.7 Sections to be covered by preview after overview. Again, add any appropriate information or references you find to your Mind Map

The essential 'mind tools' for great brains

Having an action plan, a strategy for study, is vital. A case in point is that of a student at Cambridge who had spent four months struggling through a 500-page tome on psychology. By the time he had reached page 450 he was beginning to despair because the amount of information that he was 'holding on to' as he tried to get to the end was becoming too much – he was literally beginning to drown in the information just before reaching his goal.

It transpired that he had been reading straight through the book and, even though he was nearing the end, did not know what the last chapter was about. It was a complete summary of the book!

He read the final chapter and estimated that, had he done so at the beginning, he would have saved himself approximately 70 hours reading time, 20 hours note taking time and a few hundred hours of worrying.

In both the overview and preview, you should very actively select and reject. Many people still feel obliged to read everything in a book, even though they know that it is not necessarily relevant to them. It is far better to treat a book in the way most people treat lecturers. In other words, if the lecturer is boring, skip what he or she says and, if he or she is giving too many examples, missing the point or making errors, select, criticise, correct and disregard as appropriate.

Inview

After the overview and preview, and providing that still more information is required, *inview* the material.

This involves 'filling in' those areas still left and can be compared to the filling-in part of doing a jigsaw puzzle, once the boundaries and main coloured areas have been established. It is not necessarily the major reading as, in some cases, most of the important material will have been covered in the previous stages.

Jumping over stumbling blocks

It should be noted from Figure 12.8, there are still certain sections that have been left incomplete, even at the inview stage. That is because it is far better to move over particularly difficult points than batter away at them immediately from one side only.

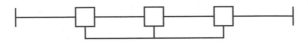

Difficult areas or areas where knowledge not complete

Figure 12.8 Sections covered after inview has been completed. As you proceed, add the relevant information to your Mind Map

Once again, the jigsaw puzzle analogy helps here. Racking your brain to find the pieces that connect to your 'difficult bit' is a tension-producing waste of time, and jamming the piece in or cutting it with a pair of scissors so that it does fit (that is, assuming or pretending you understand it in context when really you don't) is similarly futile. The difficult sections of a study text are seldom essential to that which follows them and the advantages of leaving them are manifold (see Figure 12.9).

- If they are not immediately struggled with, your brain is given a most important brief period in which it can work on them subconsciously. Most of us have experienced an examination question that we couldn't possibly answer, only to find on returning to it later, the answer pops into our minds and often seems ridiculously simple.

- If the difficult areas are returned to later, they can be approached from both sides. Considering the difficult area in context (like a difficult bit in a jigsaw) also enables your brain's automatic tendency to fill in gaps to work to greater advantage.

- Moving on from a difficult area releases the tension and mental floundering that often accompanies the traditional approach.

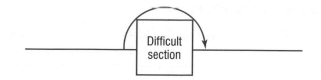

Figure 12.9 Jumping over a stumbling block usually enables you to go back to it later on with more information from 'the other side'. The block itself is seldom essential to understanding that which follows it

The great leap forward

Looking at the normal historical development of any discipline, we find that a fairly regular series of small and logically connected steps are interrupted by great leaps forward (see Figure 12.10). The propounders of these giant new steps have, in many cases, 'intuited' them (combining left- and right-brain functions) and afterwards been met with scorn. Galileo and Einstein are examples. As they then explained their ideas step by step, others gradually and progressively understood – some early on in their explanation and others as they neared their conclusions.

In the same manner that an innovator jumps over an enormous number of sequential steps and in the same way those who first realise the innovator's conclusions are valid, students who leave out small sections of study will allow their natural creative and understanding abilities a far greater range than students who don't do so.

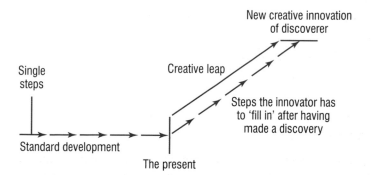

Figure 12.10 The historical development of ideas and creative innovations

Review

Having completed the overview, preview and inview and when further information is still required to achieve the goal you've set yourself, answer questions or solve problem areas, then a review stage is necessary.

For this stage, simply fill in all those areas as yet incomplete and reconsider those sections you marked as noteworthy. In most cases, you will find that not much more than 70 per cent of that initially considered relevant will finally be used.

Notes on note taking and making

Noting while studying takes two main forms:

- notes made on the text itself
- a growing Mind Map (see Chapter 9).

Notes you make in the textbook itself can include:

- underlining or highlighting
- personal thoughts generated by the text
- critical comments
- sidelining important or noteworthy material in the margin (see Figure 12.11)
- curved or wavy side-lines in the margin to indicate unclear or difficult material (see Figure 12.11)
- question marks for areas that you wish to question or find questionable
- exclamation marks for outstanding items
- your own symbols and codes for items and areas that relate to your own specific and general objectives.

The essential 'mind tools' for great brains

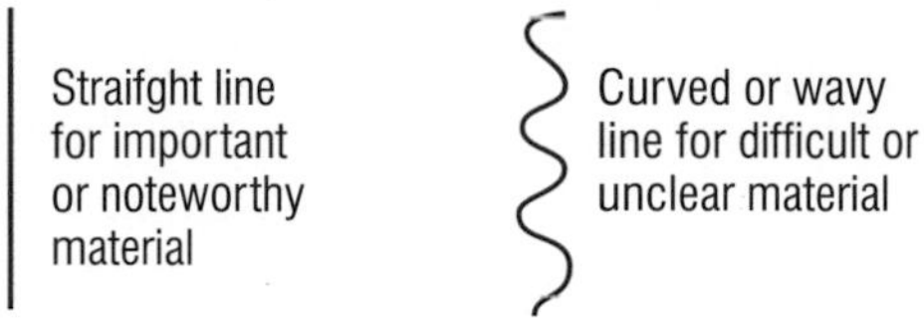

| Straifght line for important or noteworthy material | Curved or wavy line for difficult or unclear material |

Figure 12.11 Sidelining marks used for text

If the textbook is not valuable, markings can be made according to your own colour code. If the book is a cherished volume or a library book, you can use sticky notes for comments or write in very soft pencil. If the pencil is soft enough and if a very soft eraser is used, the damage to the book will be less than that caused by your finger and thumb as they turn a page (how you can use Mind Maps for this application stage is explained in the box below and in Chapter 9).

Note taking and note making using Mind Maps

You will find that Mind Mapping the structure of a text as you progress through it is a highly accessible study tool and very similar to building up the picture in a jigsaw puzzle as you fit in bit by bit. To learn how to develop and draw your own Mind Maps for different aspects of study, see Chapter 9.

The advantage of building up a Mind Map as you progress through a study text is that you externalise and integrate a lot of information that would otherwise be up in the air. The growing Mind Map also allows you to refer back quickly to areas that you have covered previously rather than have to thumb through pages that you've already read. It enables you, after a reasonable amount of basic study, to see just where any areas of confusion for you are and where your subject connects with other subjects. As such, it places you in the creative situation of being able to:

▶

- integrate the known

- realise its relevance to other areas

- make appropriate comment where confusion and debate still exist.

And finally ...

The final stage of your study will include the completion and integration of any notes from your text with your Mind Map, which will act as your basis for ongoing study and review.

When you have completed this final stage, you should – as did our imaginary jigsaw puzzle fanatic – celebrate! That may sound funny, but it is also serious. If you associate the completion of study tasks with celebration, you give your study a pleasant context and, thus, the probability of your studying in the future is far greater than if you associate it with a feeling of dread.

Once your study is well under way, it is advisable to keep large *master* Mind Maps that summarise and overview the main branches and structures of your subject areas.

Continuing review

Apart from the review at the end of your study period, outlined above, a continuing review programme is essential and should be constructed in the light of what you learned concerning memory in Chapter 5. We know that memory does not decline immediately after a learning situation – it actually *rises* before levelling off and then plummeting (see Figure 12.12).

This graph can be warped to your advantage by reviewing *just* at that point where your memory starts to fall. A review then, at the point of highest memory and integration, will keep the high point up for another one or two days, when you can review again.

*Figure 12.12 **Graph showing that memory actually rises after learning, before declining sharply***

Summary of BOST

The entire BOST programme is not as a step-by-step progression, but a series of interrelated aspects of approaching study material linked to the other chapters in this book. Remember also that it is quite possible to switch and change the order of the steps – you don't have to use the one given here.

So, for example, the amount to be covered may be decided on before the period of time; the subject matter may be known before the time and amount are decided on and, consequently, the knowledge Mind Map could be completed first; the questions can be asked at the preparation stage or after any one of the latter stages; the overview can be eliminated for books where it is inappropriate, or repeated a number of times if the subjects are mathematics or physics (one student found that it was easier to read quickly 4 chapters of post-degree mathematics 25 times per week for 4 weeks, using the survey technique, than it was to struggle through one formula at a time – he was, of course, applying to its extreme, but very effectively, the point made about skipping over difficult areas); preview can be eliminated or broken down into separate sections; and the inview and review can be variously extended or eliminated.

In other words, each subject, and each book on each subject, can be confidently approached in the manner best suited to it. To each textbook, though, you will bring the knowledge that, whatever the difficulties, you possess the fundamental understanding to choose the appropriate and necessarily unique approach for it.

Your study, consequently, is made a personal, interactive, continually changing and stimulating experience rather than a rigid, impersonal and tiresomely onerous task. It should also be noted that, despite the apparently greater number of 'times the book is being read' that is not the case. By using BOST you will, on average, be reading most sections once only and will then be effectively reviewing those sections considered important (see Figure 12.13).

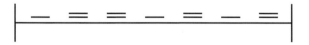

Figure 12.13 The number of times a book is covered using BOST

By contrast, traditional, 'once through' readers are not reading it once through but reading it an enormous number of times. They think that they are reading it through once only because they take in once piece of information after another. They do not realise that their regressions, back skipping, rereading of difficult sentences, general disorganisation and forgetting because of inadequate review result in an actual reading of the book or chapter as many as ten times (see Figure 12.14).

Figure 12.14 The number of times a book is covered using traditional 'once through' reading techniques

BOST – in tandem with speed reading, Mind Maps, memory skills and creative thinking already covered in the book – allows you easy and effective access to the world of knowledge in a manner that will encourage your brain to learn more, and more easily, as it learns a

The essential 'mind tools' for great brains

vaster array of knowledge. It will turn you from a reluctant learner into one who will avidly devour books, course texts and manuals, presentations and seminars by the hundred!

Next, let us look at the great opportunities that await those of you who are now going to *use your head* to harness the innovative learning and thinking techniques I have devised to help you succeed in the century of the brain, millennium of the mind and the age of intelligence.

Conclusion: Thinking for the future

As the twenty-first century (the century of the brain) and the third millennium (the millennium of the mind) dawned, the human race, with many members still not realising it, entered what will probably be considered by future historians as the beginning of the greatest renaissance ever – one that will arguably become a permanent feature of human evolution. That renaissance is the age of intelligence.

The age of intelligence

In the 40 years since I first wrote *Use Your Head*, there has been a worldwide explosion in our fascination with, as well as an accelerating investigation of, our own intelligence. The age of intelligence has been ushered in by an explosive growth in brain research, a growing global fascination with the brain and its extraordinary capacities and the increasing appearance of the brain in all forms of media, especially magazines.

Up until 1991, as far as our records show, no magazine had featured the brain on its front cover. The first magazine to do so (and it was as recently as 1991) was *Fortune Magazine*, when its front cover proclaimed, 'Brainpower: How Intellectual Capital is Becoming America's Most Valuable Asset'. In other words, if you want to make a fortune, invest in your brain.

The *Fortune Magazine* article opened the floodgates and thousands of magazines featured the brain on front covers that had previously devoted themselves to various physical and human objects of desire. Here are a few examples.

Time, which has fallen in love with the brain, having featured it on over 20 covers, has focused on creativity, memory and the astonishing new finding that the intelligence of our brains is intricately connected to the way in which they have been nurtured, including the astonishing revelation that our physical brain continues to grow if nurtured appropriately and will disintegrate if not nurtured well.

Scientific American's new magazine, *Mind*, featured an entire issue devoted to creativity and innovation. The heading on the front page proclaimed, 'How Brilliance Arises in Every One of Us'. In other words, the global scientific community has come to the unanimous conclusion that *everyone* is fundamentally brilliant and it is our responsibility to nurture and harvest that brilliance. *The Economist* has picked up on this in our social and cultural context with its 2009 special quarterly *Intelligent Life* and an article entitled 'The Age of Mass Intelligence'.

Review, mental ability and age

Old beliefs are disintegrating in the glare of our knowledge about ourselves. Take, for example, ideas about the way in which human mental abilities decline with age. The way in which a person reviews has an interesting connection with popular ideas about this.

It is normally assumed that IQ scores, recall ability, ability to see special relationships, perceptual speed, speed of judgement, induction, figural relations, associative memory, intellectual level, intellectual speed, semantic relations, formal and general reasoning, decline after reaching a peak at the age of 18 to 25 (see Figure C.1). Valid as Figure C.1 may be, two important factors must be noted.

- The decline that takes place over a lifetime is little more than 5 to 10 per cent. When considered in relation to your brain's enormous inherent capacity, that is insignificant.

- The people who took part in the experiments and produced these discouraging figures had been educated traditionally, so, in most cases, would not have been practising proper learning, reviewing and remembering techniques.

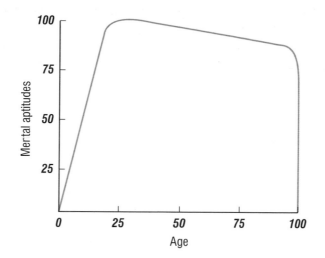

Figure C.1 **Graph showing the standard results when measuring mental aptitudes as a person gets older. It is assumed that, after reaching a peak at approximately 18 to 25, decline is thereafter slow but steady**

Looking at the graph in Figure C.1, it is easy to see that such people's mental 'conditioning' would have been at a very low level for an increasing number of years. In other words, their real intellectual capacities would have been in 'cold storage'. It is not surprising, then, that such unused minds would do slightly worse after 20 to 40 years of mis- or no use – it is surprising that they still manage to do as well as they do!

If, alternatively, your mind is being continually used and its capacities expanded, the effect on the graph would be dramatic (see Figure C.2). This can be seen by taking note of those older people who have remained active and explorative rather than assuming that they would get worse as the years passed. Very often, their recall is almost total and their ability to understand and learn new areas of knowledge far surpasses that of equally enthusiastic but younger and less experienced minds.

When studying human mental performance, it has been mistakenly assumed that the decline found with age is 'natural' and unavoidable. Instead, a closer look should be taken at the people being studied, then experiments should be performed to find out how their mental abilities can be maximised rather than minimised.

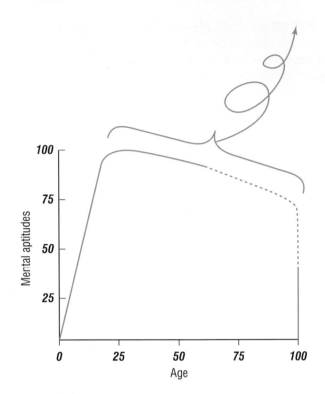

Figure C.2 **Graphs such as that shown in Figure C.1 are based on statistics from people taught traditionally. People would naturally tend to improve their capacities with age if taught in a manner that complemented and nourished the brain's natural functioning**

Increasingly, we are finding positive 'renegades from the norm' – that is, people over the age of 70, 80 and even 90 whose defining characteristics are vitality, optimism, humour, physical strength, persistence, mischievousness, enthusiasm, interest, expanding knowledge, curiosity, kindness, exhaustive memory and sensuality. The very characteristics that we would ascribe to children.

The explosion in brain training games, including those by global giants such as Nintendo, also points to a growing awareness of the fact that mental stimulation is not age-restricted. Indeed, the conviction now is that your brain can be tuned to maximum sharpness, just as physical health and fitness can be transformed through diet and exercise. Whether doing these kinds of things can blunt the effects of, or ward off the threat of, dementia and Alzheimer's disease or not is under the critical eye of much current neuroscience research.

We are finding that, if we understand, care for and use our heads in the way that they were designed, the 'Edward Hughes story' will become the 'every child story'.

Looking forward

Having worked your way through this book, your mental armoury is now complete and you are re-equipped with a brain of extraordinary power. You have obliterated the standard obstacles to effective learning. You are able to read faster than 99 per cent of the population and you have a newly supercharged and harnessed mcmory. You have knowledge of the theory and application of the ultimate thinking, learning, and memory tool – the Mind Map – and know how to mobilise the most powerful studying technique – BOST – to your ultimate advantage.

To maximise your already amazing brain's potential, I leave you with ten simple guidelines to using *Use Your Head*.

1   **Develop your multiple intelligences**. These include your creative intelligence, personal intelligence, social intelligence, ethical/spriritual intelligence, physical intelligence, verbal intelligence, mathematical intelligence, spatial intelligence and sensual intelligence. These multiple intelligences, which we all have, are your 'universal survival kit' and are the 'body of your mind', which can grow in strength just like your physical body.

2   **Physically fit = brain fit**. The old adage *Mens sana in corpore sano* – healthy body, healthy mind; healthy mind, healthy body – is true. When you are physically fit, you will be more mentally fit and vice versa. For instance, when you are aerobically conditioned, your brain receives more and more 'Formula 1' blood, every *second* of your life.

3   **Mind Map!** The Mind Map is your Swiss army knife for your brain. Use it and your brain will be much more accomplished, much more in control and much more happier!

4   **Develop your memory**. Your memory, in many ways, is who you are. Think of what it would be like if your entire memory

was taken away from you. Read books, scan the Web, enter memory competitions, learn memory techniques and attend memory improving courses. When you do, your life will be a much more enjoyable and *memorable one!*

5   **Play mind sports**. Stimulate your short-term memory and boost your long-term memory. *Use Your Head* celebrates the five sports of the mind – memory, speed reading, IQ, creativity and Mind Mapping – and you should also get involved with games such as chess and Go, as well as brain skill sports, such as puzzles and brainteasers. Such mind sports have been found to stimulate many areas of the brain and reduce the chance of the onset of Alzheimer's. Your brain is designed to learn throughout your life. Keep it stimulated by learning new and varied subjects throughout your life and make sure you Mind Map what you learn.

6   **Feed your mind**. There is a simple slogan to help you focus on this: GF, GB; JF, JB. It stands for 'good food, good brain; junk food, junk brain'. As your brain is the prime recipient of the food you eat, make sure that the food you eat is of the highest nutritional quality.

7   **Live your life vision**. People with a major purpose or vision are found to have more energy, be more positive, have healthier immune systems and live longer than those who don't. With the help of family and friends, define and Mind Map your life vision and pursue it with energy and enthusiasm.

8   **Take regular breaks**. Your brain and body need regular breaks in order to recuperate and to integrate what has gone before. Schedule such breaks (as discussed in Chapter 4) – whether they be walks in nature, hot baths or listening to your favourite music – as a matter of course.

9   **Seek solitude sometimes**. You need time to be on your own. It gives you the opportunity for conversations that are among the most important you will ever have: conversations with yourself. Plan to give yourself solitude.

10 **Take emotional nourishment**. The flipside of solitude is also important and many scientific studies have shown that when

your brain is fed the 'food' of friendship, affection and love, it flowers and flourishes. Make sure that you get and give ample doses of all!

As you approach the end of *Use Your Head*, I hope that you will be realising it is not the end, but the real beginning. You can now:

- appreciate the physical beauty and complexity of your brain

- understand your brain's enormous intellectual and emotional powers

- realise that you are able to absorb information and manage to memorise that information

- allow your brain to express and organise itself in matters that are more comprehensibly attuned to the way you function than before, by using the new techniques you have leaned.

Reading, studying, learning and life in general should, from here on, become what they can be – delightful and flowing processes that bring pleasure and fulfilment. Enjoy using your head for the rest of your life!

Appendix: Online resources

Anyone interested in reading more or in courses dealing with the subjects covered in *Use Your Head* can contact the author via ThinkBuzan.

There you will enter Tony Buzan's world. As you know, Tony Buzan is the inventor of Mind Maps – the most powerful 'thinking tool' of our times. Discover more about Tony himself and the transformative powers of Mind Mapping, memory and speed reading at **www.thinkbuzan.com**

Mind Mapping software

ThinkBuzan.com   ThinkBuzan is the new company incorporating Buzan Online and the Buzan Organisation, with CEO Chris Griffiths at the helm, appointed by his friend and colleague Tony Buzan. ThinkBuzan has become the welcome home to iMindMap, Mind Mapping and more.

ThinkBuzan is set to bring Mind Mapping to a larger audience and improve global mental literacy. Tony Buzan was delighted to appoint Chris Griffiths, CEO of Buzan Online, as the CEO of ThinkBuzan to help develop and revolutinise this new era of thinking. By combining the enthusiasm and talent of both teams, Tony's vision of Mind Mapping is certain to strengthen and grow around the world.

This powerful union is reflected by the new ThinkBuzan website. The new website, **www.thinkbuzan.com**, is the culmination of the stregthened Mind Mapping vision and is home to a wealth of diverse products. The website hosts the original iMindMap desktop software, the iMindMap Mobile and iPad app, the full library of books by Tony Buzan and an enhanced range of training courses, many led by Tony Buzan himself.

The website is vibrant, flexible and easy to use – a testament to the principles of Mind Mapping, creativity and innovation. With easy navigation, bold colours, key words and headings, the new website also offers a range of new pages bound to inspire and motivate:

To see the new website for yourself, please visit **www.thinkbuzan.com**

To aid you in your search for relevant memory, Mind Mapping, speed reading, BOST and other creativity stimuli, below are the websites currently associated with Tony Buzan and his Festival of the Mind, with brief explanations.

The Festival of the Mind

This is a showcase event for the five learning mind sports of memory, speed reading, IQ, creativity and Mind Mapping (see **www.festivalofthemind.com** for more information).

The first festival was held in the Royal Albert Hall in 1995 and organised by Tony Buzan and Raymond Keene, OBE. Since then, the festival has been held in the UK, alongside the World Memory Championships in Oxford, and in other countries around the world, including Malaysia, China and Bahrain. The interest from the public in all five learning mind sports is growing worldwide so, not surprisingly, the festival is a big attraction. In fact, an event devoted solely to Mind Maps with Tony Buzan filled the Albert Hall again in 2006.

Each of the mind sports has its own council to promote, administer and recognise achievement in its field.

The World Memory Sports Council

WORLD MEMORY SPORTS COUNCIL The council is the independent governing body of the mind sport of memory and regulates competitions worldwide. Tony Buzan is president of the council. You can visit the council's website at **www.worldmemorysportscouncil.com**

The World Memory Championships

This is the pre-eminent national and international memory competition where records are continuously smashed. For instance, in the 2007 UK Memory Championships, Ben Pridmore memorised a single shuffled deck of playing cards in 26.28 seconds, beating the previous world record of 31.16 seconds set by Andi Bell. For years, memorising a pack of cards in under 30 seconds has been seen as the memory equivalent of beating the 4-minute mile in athletics. Full details of the World Memory Championships can be found on its website at **www.worldmemorychampionships. com**, with its interactive Mind Map designed by Mind Map world champion Phil Chambers using Buzan's iMind Map software.

The UK Schools Memory Championships

Since it was founded in 1991, the World Memory Championships has created a gold standard for memory based on ten different memory disciplines. A simplified version has now been created specially for schools memory competitions, backed up with a training programme to help teachers teach memory techniques.

In a nationwide educational partnership, consisting of the UK Memory Sports Council, Inspire Education and national government initiative Aimhigher, students are taught powerful memory techniques that, when put into practice, can provide the intellectual platform for recalling almost anything, instantly. They are passing on these techniques to teachers and pupils at secondary schools throughout the UK, by means of the UK Schools Memory Championships.

Organised by Inspire Education and spearheaded by eight-times world memory champion, Dominic O'Brien, and the chief arbiter of the World Memory Championships, Phil Chambers, the UK Schools Memory Championships has been created to help pupils discover the mind sport of memory and develop their mental skills to help them with their studies. We are in the process of creating a model here in the UK that can be repeated around the world, with the goal of eventually establishing the World Schools Memory Championships soon after 2010. For more information, log on to **www.schoolsmemorychampionships.com**

The World Speed Reading Council

The council was established to promote, train and recognise achievements in the field of speed reading worldwide.

Apart from developing the ability to gain an understanding of large quantities of text in a short time, speed reading is one of the five learning mind sports that can be practised competitively. The council's website is at **www.worldspeedreadingcouncil.com**

The World Mind Mapping Council

The World Mind Mapping Council administers and promotes the sport of Mind Mapping, invented by Tony Buzan in 1971, and also awards the prestigious title of Mind Mapping world champion. The current reigning world champion is Phil Chambers. Visit the council's website at **www.worldmindmappingcouncil.com**

The Worldwide Brain Club

Set up by the Buzan Organization, the club encourages the formation of brain clubs worldwide. The clubs have flourished for many years and bring together Mind Mapping, creativity, IQ, speed reading and memory. Practising each of these disciplines positively impacts the others. Using Mind Maps, for example, helps with creativity as it presents ideas in a brain-friendly way that inspires new ideas. Working on memory techniques makes your brain more capable in every other area, in the same way that working out in a gym builds your muscles and fitness.

Brain clubs, whether set up in a school or college or within an organisation or company, create a supportive environment where all their members share the same objective: to give their personal 'necktop computer' the best operating system possible. Buzan Centres Worldwide provide qualified trainers in all of these areas. Visit **www.thinkbuzan.com** and **www.worldbrainclub.com** for more information.

The Brain Trust

The trust is a registered charity that was founded in 1990 by Tony Buzan with one objective: to maximise the ability of each and every individual to unlock and deploy the vast capacity of his or her brain. Its charter includes promoting research into the study of thought processes, and the investigation of the mechanics of thinking, manifested in learning, understanding, communication, problem solving, creativity and decisionmaking. In 2008, Baroness Professor Susan Greenfield, CBE, won its 'Brain of the Century' award. Visit **www.braintrust.org.uk** for more information.

The International Academy of Mental World Records

The Academy exists to recognise the achievements of mental athletes around the world. In addition to arbitrating world record attempts and awarding certificates of achievement, the Academy is also linked to the Festival of the Mind International, which showcases mental achievements in the five learning mind sports of memory, speed reading, creativity, Mind Mapping and IQ. For more information, visit its webiste at **www.mentalworldrecords.com**

The World Creativity Council

Creativity is defined by E. Paul Torrance, the doyen of creativity testing, as follows:

Creativity is a process of becoming sensitive to problems, deficiencies, gaps in knowledge, missing elements, disharmonies and so on; identifying the difficulty; searching for solutions; making guesses or formulating hypotheses about the deficiencies; testing and re-testing these hypotheses and possibly modifying and retesting them; and finally communicating the results.

Creativity is one of the five learning mind sports along with Mind Mapping, speed reading, IQ and memory. All these skills positively impact the others and, together, can help any individual to be more effective in whatever they choose to do. All five learning mind sports are featured in the Festival of the Mind International. Visit **www.worldcreativitycouncil.com** for more information.

The World IQ Council

IQ is one of the five learning mind sports, the others being Mind Mapping, creativity, speed reading and memory.

The World IQ Council can be contacted at **www.worldiqcouncil.com** and you can also test your IQ on this website.

Index

age
  creativity studies xiv–xv
  memory 41–2
  mental ability 192–5
alphabet method (reading) 144
alphabet systems (memory) 76
Anokhin, Pyotr 23–4
application strategy, BOST 169
  continuing review 186–7
  inview step 181–3
  overview step 175–9
  preview step 179–81
  review step 184–5
associations
  brain processes 4–6
  creativity 85–7
  imagination 78
  learning 47, 48
  Mind Maps 63
  mnemonics 60
  words 102

babies, development of 33–4
Basic Ordering Ideas (BOIs)
        118–19, 124
Berkeley Study on Creativity 27
Binet, Alfred 27, 28
BOST (Buzan Organic Study
        Technique) 115
  application strategy 169, 175–86
  exams, fear of 161
  information explosion 163–4
  mental blocks 164–6
  preparation strategy 169–74
  reading techniques, BOST versus
        traditional 188
  'reluctant learner' 161–4

study, personal and interactive
        187–8
study techniques, outdated
        166–9
brain
  associations 4–6
  branching association machine
        (BAM) 5–6
  complexity of 5–6
  creative thinking 85–9
  human mind, current knowledge
        of 6–7
  location of 6
  true potential of xii–xiv, 6–13,
        23–4
brain structure
  cerebral cortex 15–17, 114–15
  hologram model 25–6
  Mind Maps 109, 110, 119–21
  neurons 18, 20
  perception, models of 24–5
  physical characteristics 15, 20
Brain Trust, The 202
breaks, need for 49–51, 196
Buzan Organic Study Technique
        see BOST (Buzan Organic
        Study Technique)

cerebral cortex
  cerebral processes 15
  cognitive skills of 88
  corpus callosum 15
  left and right cortex, dominant
        processes of 16, 18, 19, 59,
        85, 114–15
  lopsided versus whole-brained
        development 16–17

Chambers, Phil 119, 201
colour 65, 123–4, 185
cramming 169
creative thinking
    age xiv–xv
    associations 85–7
    brain hemispheres, left and right
        85
    creative breakthroughs 78
    creative capital 78
    daydreaming 84–5
    dedication 78–9
    exercises 80–3
    flexibility 88
    great leap forward 183
    imagination 78, 85
    increasing xv–xvi
    intelligences, multiple 31, 32, 88
    key words 99, 101–4
    Leonardo da Vinci on 78–9
    locations for 83–4
    memory 77–8
    originality 87–8
    practice of 88–9
    'reluctant learner' 164
    solutions 78
    thinking at speed 87
    volume, production of 88

da Vinci, Leonardo 17, 31, 78–9
daydreaming 84–5

Einstein, Albert 16–17, 64
emotional nourishment 196–7
ethical intelligence 31, 32
exams
    education system 164–5
    'failing' 165–6
    fear of 161, 165
eye movements (reading)
    aided versus unaided 151–2
    assumed movements 146–8,
        149–50
    concentration 150
    fixations, increasing size of 147,
        149–50

groups of words, focusing on
        149
    human eye, design of 145, 154
    skipping back, avoiding 147
    slow readers 147
    speeding up 147–8
Eysenck, Hans 31

Festival of the Mind xiv, 199
fitness, physical 10, 195
five minute jotter 172–3
Fortune Magazine 191

Gardner, Howard 31–3
Gestalt psychology 16, 170–1
great leap forward 183
Greenfield, Susan 202
Griffiths, Chris 199

hemispheres, left and right of brain
        see cerebral cortex
hologram model, of brain 25–6
Hughes, Edward, story of
    background 8–9
    Edward Hughes today 12–13
    exam results 10, 12
    'I will get an A' 9–10
    study schedule 10–11

imagination
    creative thinking 78, 85
    memory 61, 64–5, 67
    Mind Maps 65
iMindMap software 119, 123, 136,
        138, 198
information explosion 139, 163–4
information management xvii
intelligence, age of xvii, 191–2
intelligences, multiple
    case study 29–31
    creative intelligence 31, 32, 88
    development of 195
    ethical/spiritual intelligence 31,
        32
    human body, as model of
        excellence 33–4

human brain, 'reining in' of 34–6
Mind Map of 33
numerical intelligence 31, 32
'only human', mistakes as 36–8
personal intelligence 31, 32
physical intelligence 31, 32
sensual intelligence 31, 32
social intelligence 31, 32
spatial intelligence 31, 32
verbal intelligence 31, 32
see also creative thinking; IQ
    tests
Intelligent Life 192
International Academy of Mental
    World Records, The 202
IQ tests 27–8
    see also intelligences, multiple

key words
    choice of 98–9
    main and secondary 93, 97–8,
        99
    Mind Maps 99, 100, 107
    recall versus creative 99, 101–4
    words, multiordinate nature of
        102–4
kinaesthesia 62

language, complexity of learning
    34
learning
    core skills inherent in xvi
    individuals, focus on 168–9
    subjects, focus on 167–9
linear thinking
    note taking 111, 112
    print 111, 112, 114
    speech, and brain processes
        111–14, 119
    versus whole-brain thinking
        114–15
link system (memory) 76

memory
    age 41–2
    creativity 77–8

development of 195–6
feats of 59–60
key words 106
long-term, transfer to 57
Mind Maps, for reviews 55
reading 142
repetition 20–1, 47, 48, 57
review 55–8
training, benefits of 60–1
versus understanding 41, 46–9,
    50
see also mnemonics; recall
Memory Book, The (Buzan) 74, 76
Mind 192
Mind Map Book, The (Buzan) 119,
    136
Mind Map creation
    Buzan CV Mind Maps 126, 127
    colour, using 123–4
    core question 123
    curved lines, using 124
    economics notes, GCSE student
        130–1
    empty branches, adding 125
    English notes, schoolboy 130
    goal, and central image 123
    key words, adding 124
    mathematics notes, A level
        student 132, 133
    memorability 132, 136
    natural laws 128
    paper orientation 123
    pauses, avoiding 128
    primary branching 124
    second/third level branches,
        adding 125
    steps for 123–9
    'synaesthesia' Mind Map 134
    whole-brain thinking Mind Map
        134
Mind Maps
    associations 63
    Basic Ordering Ideas (BOIs)
        118–19, 124
    brain structure 109, 110, 119–21
    creative thinking 84

Mind Maps (*continued*)
  essay practice 9, 11–12
  imagination 65
  initial ideas 119
  key images 115–16
  key words 115–16
  linear thinking 111–15
  memory triggers 109
  natural structures 110
  as philosophy of life 90
  positive thinking 66
  problem-solving 129
  Radiant Thinking 116–17
  senses/sensuality 62
  software for 109, 119, 123, 136, 138, 198
  space travel exercise 10, 110
  uses of xvii, 13, 110, 136–8
Mind Maps for Business (Buzan) 136, 138
mind sports 196, 199
mind tools xvi, 91–2
  key words 93–107
  note taking 104–7
mnemonics
  acronyms 60
  association 61, 63, 71–2, 75
  brain functioning 59, 60–1
  creativity 78
  face-name system 74
  I AM mnemonic 67
  imagination 61
  'impossible task' case study 75–6
  major system 74
  number-rhyme system 68–74
  number-shape system 74
  SMASHIN SCOPE mnemonic 61–7
multiple intelligences *see* intelligences, multiple

neurons
  axons 18
  cell body 18
  dendrites 18
  synaptic connections 18, 20

note taking
  BOST, preview step 180
  colour coding 185
  key concept overviews 104
  key words 104, 106, 107
  Mind Maps, using 185–6
  order-of-importance-based 111, 112
  review graph 56, 107
  sentence-based 111, 112
  sidelining marks 184–5
  traditionally 'good' 104–6
number-rhyme system (memory) 76
number-shape system (memory) 76
numerical intelligence 28, 31, 32

O'Brien, Dominic 7, 38, 61, 201
online resources
  Brain Trust, The 202
  Festival of the Mind, The 199
  iMind Map, Mind Mapping 198
  International Academy of Mental World Records, The 202
  Think Buzan website 198–9
  UK Schools Memory Championships 200–1
  World Creativity Council, The 203
  World IQ Council, The 203
  World Memory Sports Championships, The 200
  World Memory Sports Council, The 200
  World Mind Mapping Council, The 201
  World Speed Reading Council, The 201
  Worldwide Brain Club, The 201–2
Ornstein, Robert 16

peg system (memory) 76
perception, models of 24–5
Persistence of Memory, The (Dali) 64
personal intelligence 31, 32

physical intelligence 31, 32
preparation strategy, BOST
   browse 170
   five minute jotter 172–3
   questions and goals 173–4
   time and amount decisions
      170–2
Presidents Club, Cambridge 10
Pridmore, Ben 7, 61
primacy effect 47, 49

Radiant Thinking 116–17
reading
   assimilation 142, 145
   assumptions about 139–50
   communication 142
   comprehension 142, 145
   environmental influences 156–7
   initial teaching methods 144–5
   mastering 142, 143, 144
   peripheral vision, use of 154
   reasons for 144–5
   recall 142
   recognition 141, 145
   retention 142
   techniques, BOST *versus*
      traditional 188
   understanding 142
   visual guide, using 151–2, 178–9
   see also eye movements; speed
      reading
recall
   after learning 41, 51–4
   age 41–2
   breaks, need for 49–51
   information, accessing 41–2
   during learning 41–51
   learning periods, length of 49
   memory *versus* understanding
      41, 46–9, 50
   review techniques and theory
      55–8
recency effect 47, 49
repetition 20–1, 47, 48, 57
rhythm, and mental pictures 63

Scientific American 19?
sensual intelligence 31, 32
skim reading 180
SMASHIN SCOPE mnemonic
      technique
   senses/sensuality 62
   movement 63
   associations 63
   sexuality 64
   humour 64
   imagination 64–5
   number 65
   symbolism 65
   colour 65
   order and/or sequence 66
   positivity 66
   exaggeration 66–7
   and Mind Map structure 67
social intelligence 31, 32
software, for Mind Maps 119, 123,
      136, 138, 198
solitude, need for 196
solution-finding mechanism, brain
      as 83
spatial intelligence 28, 31, 32
speed reading 150
   as core skill 139
   metronome training 159
   motivational practice 156
   perception, high speed 155
   speed test 158
   visual focus, expansion of 153–4
   see also reading
Sperry, Roger 16
spiritual intelligence 31, 32
study techniques
   individual to subjects 168–9
   subjects to individual 166–8
   see also BOST (Buzan Organic
      Study Technique)
supercomputer, brain as 5–6
synaesthesia 62, 134

textbooks
   education system, exam-based
      164–5

textbooks (*continued*)
    study techniques 167
    see also BOST (Buzan Organic
        Study Technique); study
        techniques
The Economist 192
Think Buzan website 198–9
Time 192
Torrence, E. Paul 80

UK Schools Memory
        Championships 200–1
understanding, *versus* remembering
    41, 46–9, 50
Use Your Head (Buzan) 75, 191,
    195–7
    see also Hughes, Edward

verbal intelligence 28, 31, 32
vision, living 196
visual aids, and reading 151–2,
    178–9
Von Restorff effect 47, 49

words *see* key words
World Creativity Council, The 203
World IQ Council, The 204
World Memory Championships 7,
    61
World Memory Sports
    Championships, The 200
World Memory Sports Council, The
    199
World Mind Mapping Council, The
    201
World Speed Reading Council, The
    201
Worldwide Brain Club, The 201–2

Young Entrepreneurs Society,
    Cambridge 10

Zaidel, Eran 16

Unleash the power of your mind with these bestselling titles from the world's leading authority on the brain and learning...

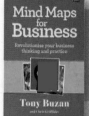

Mind Maps for Business
Revolutionise your business thinking and practice
Tony Buzan
and Chris Griffiths

ISBN 9781406642902

Unlock the power of your brain to transform your business practice and performance with the ultimate 21st Century business tool – the Mind Map.

The Mind Map Book
Unlock your creativity, boost your memory, change your life
Tony Buzan

ISBN 9781406647167

The original and the best book on Mind Maps from their world-renowned inventor.

The Memory Book
Boost your memory, year after year
Tony Buzan

ISBN 9781406644265

Embark on the most exciting intellectual adventure of your life and discover how easy it is to supercharge your memory.

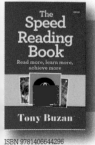

The Speed Reading Book
Read more, learn more, achieve more
Tony Buzan

ISBN 9781406644296

Revolutionise the way you read with the ultimate guide to reading, understanding and learning at amazing speeds.